What people are saying about

Wisdom for Living

If there's a life situation not addressed in this book, I sure can't find it! The short essay-meditations use the topics to draw out the already-present wisdom in the reader. Through personal, engaging and often humorous reflections, they provoked, delighted and enlightened me throughout. This collection is a wonderful addition to the world's wisdom, and a portable friend on life's remarkable journey.
Cliff Penwell, Founder, OriginalVoice

This lovely book is packed with jewels of wisdom that will surely make your life more rewarding as you put them into practice. I especially enjoyed the exercises offered. Take advantage of the gifts bestowed here!
Alan Cohen, author of *A Deep Breath of Life*

A feast of wisdoms awaits the readers of this book. I find this collection inspiring in a wonderfully companioning way; it's as though each entry—some expected, others surprising—begins a conversation that the reader is invited to continue in a journal. The book offers an important meeting between positive wisdoms of past and present that the reader may carry as blessings into the future.
Dr. Nancy Corson Carter, Professor of Humanities Emerita, Eckerd College, author most recently of *The Never-Quite-Ending War: A WWII GI Daughter's Stories*

A stimulating guidebook on how to live our lives wisely. The many pithy essays are like gourmet entrees—compact enough to swallow in one mouthful, rich enough to stimulate and satisfy our appetite. Erudite and homespun, practical and inspirational, these pages are brimming with pearls of reflection that open a pathway to our own inner wisdom.

Roland Evans, author of *Seeking Wholeness: Insight into the Mystery of Experience*

It seems that Reynold Feldman has been harvesting and sharing gems of wisdom forever. This multi-cultural maven has produced the Michelin Guides of Wisdom so we can stop and feast on ideas that nourish our souls. Get this book and tell the buyers at your public library to add it.

Loren Ekroth, Ph.D., author/publisher of *Better Conversations* essays, www. conversationmatters.com

Some of the quotes in this book are reminders of perennials, some are refreshing insights, some startling revelations, some beautiful prose. They comprise an intriguing variety. The authors discuss each quote with impeccable clarity, and with the guiding idea that our lives can improve only at the core when we develop and follow wisdom.

Dr. Garrett Thomson, Professor of Philosophy, College of Wooster, and Executive Director, The Guerrand-Hermès Foundation, Brighton, England

These short bits of wisdom are digestible excuses to slow down, reflect, engage with your past and enrich your present. This book is a great resource for moments when you find yourself needing to take a step back from your daily routine. Or, better yet, to assign yourself a few of the page-long wisdoms each day as a rewarding morning or evening mindfulness ritual. There is a little something for everyone.

Meredith Olsen, MBA, Marketing Professional

The authors have harvested some inspiring and wonderful adages from far and wide. A potpourri of wonderful life truths, these brief essays can startle us with their simplicity and effectiveness. A fantastic plus is how we're challenged to introspect on each "Wisdom" and enticed to personalize these in our own lives and reflections.

Saleem Ahmed, Ph.D., Founder & President, The All Believer Network (Belnet), Honolulu, Hawaii

In Feldman and Clark's WISDOM FOR LIVING, their charming and profoundly wise voices reach through the pages and dig deep into our deepest human condition, shake its cage and set us free. This book is the read our world needs.

Kate Mueth, Founder & Director, Neo-Political Cowgirls, East Hampton, New York

Drawing on many sacred and secular wisdom traditions, Feldman and Clark have managed to create an experiential process that draws readers to reflect on the many pithy quotations that are here explained in common-sense language. Even the playful alphabetical listing of topics adds a light touch to this inspiring collection.

Dr. Judith Blackburn, Professor Emerita (English and Women's Studies), Northern Kentucky University

This is a book you can thumb through for inspiration, pondering, and joy. In short takes, Feldman and Clark present wisdom from many sources, ancient and contemporary, that allows readers to cull and shape their own ideas to live by.

Sara Davidson, *NY Times* best-selling author of The December project, *Loose Change*, and *Joan: Forty Years of Life, Loss, and Friendship with Joan Didion*

Feldman and Clark's meaningful book presents wisdom as a practical guide to living. They distinguish different types of wisdom and show how, with erudite introductions and helpful exercises, wise living can be attained. The book should be read by anyone who wants to deepen his or her understanding of how to live an examined life.

Victor Margolin, Ph.D., Professor Emeritus of Design History, University of Illinois, Chicago

Wisdom for Living

Learning to Follow Your Inner Guidance

Wisdom for Living

Learning to Follow Your Inner Guidance

Reynold Ruslan Feldman
and Sharon Clark

BOOKS
Winchester, UK
Washington, USA

JOHN HUNT PUBLISHING

First published by O-Books, 2019
O-Books is an imprint of John Hunt Publishing Ltd., 3 East St., Alresford,
Hampshire SO24 9EE, UK
office@jhpbooks.net
www.johnhuntpublishing.com
www.o-books.com

For distributor details and how to order please visit the 'Ordering' section on our website.

ISBN: 978 1 78904 149 1
978 1 78904 150 7 (ebook)
Library of Congress Control Number: 2018945363

A CIP catalogue record for this book is available from the British Library.

Design: Stuart Davies

UK: Printed and bound by CPI Group (UK) Ltd, Croydon, CR0 4YY
US: Printed and bound by Thomson-Shore, 7300 West Joy Road, Dexter, MI 48130

We operate a distinctive and ethical publishing philosophy in
all areas of our business, from our global network of authors to
production and worldwide distribution.

Contents

A Warm Welcome!

Dear Reader,

Do you know how wise you are? Doubt not! In this profound book, visionary teacher and author Dr. Reynold Feldman (Ren) gathers wisdom from masters down through the ages, adds his humble and humorous wisdom, and leads you to discover your own.

One of the masters Ren quotes is philosopher Kahlil Gibran, whose seminal book, *The Prophet* (1923), states this about a teacher: "If he [sic] is indeed wise, he does not bid you enter the house of his wisdom, but rather leads you to the threshold of your own mind."

Ren is such a teacher—a nationally recognized authority on innovative education. I first heard him speak about his book, *Wisdom: Daily Reflections for a New Era*, in 2000 at a church in Honolulu. During a workshop he later presented, I was surprised at the wisdom he drew forth from me in writing exercises based on his book. In the years since, I have sporadically studied Ren's book when I had quiet time from my public-relations career to fully contemplate the day's reflection.

When I recently wanted to buy a copy of the book for a friend, I was dismayed to discover it wasn't available. In disbelief I contacted Ren and learned that when the first run of his book had sold out, the publisher switched their marketing focus, and the book went out of print. I believe that the world needs Ren's timeless wisdom more than ever, and my inner voice directed me to volunteer my assistance in having this important work updated and republished. Ren hadn't given it much thought, busy as he's been writing new books, teaching, and lecturing. He was pleased to learn of my interest, however, and our collaboration since has resulted in the book you now see.

Whenever you choose to read it, your natural wisdom will emerge as you draw on your experiences and discover insights as you reflect on your life and write your responses in a Wisdom Journal. I wish you much joy as you access your inner guidance and create your own Book of Wisdom.

Sincerely,

Sharon Clark

Introduction

In his book *The Survival of the Wisest* (1973), Dr. Jonas Salk, discoverer of the first polio vaccine, argued that world survival depended on wisdom. Wise people for him were those who made decisions that over the long term yielded positive rather than negative results. Unless enough such individuals emerged, he didn't extend the planet much hope.

As the turn of the millennium approached, some people expected imminent disaster. Others predicted the Last Days, the Second Coming, or the Rapture. Still others saw paradise arriving with each new technological breakthrough. To judge by the news media and movies, the pessimists have it. Now, 18 years into the 21st Century, the future looks uncertain and perilous. Whatever the case, the need for wisdom—for deciding appropriately what to do during our limited stay on the planet—remains front and center in our lives.

The present collection of short essays is meant to stimulate your own wisdom. At the end of each we ask you to think about some aspect of your life in light of the reading and to write your thoughts down in a Wisdom Journal (WJ). Now a Wisdom Journal is no more than a blank notebook of your choosing. Limit your writing to 10 to 15 minutes. Just write freely and leave your internal critic aside. Your Wisdom Journal is intended just for you.

This book isn't meant to add another burden to already busy lives. Each entry can be read and reread quickly. Devote, say, twenty minutes to wisdom before or after breakfast or before going to sleep. A Yugoslav proverb has it right: "Grain by grain, a loaf; stone by stone, a castle." By the time you have journaled on all the readings here, you'll be surprised by what you have created: a wisdom book of your own.

Bon voyage! May your wisdom journey introduce you to the wonderful possibility of following your own inner guidance, the inborn capacity of your biggest and best self.

Cordially,

Reynold Ruslan Feldman and Sharon Clark
New Year's Day, 2019

The Wisdom of Beginning

The beginning is the most important part of work.
— Plato (c. 427–347 BCE), *The Republic*

Welcome to an exploration of personal wisdom where you are author, protagonist, and chief beneficiary. What you do or don't do today will affect who, where, and what you are not only tomorrow but all the tomorrows thereafter. In the words of a contemporary American saying, "Today is the first day of the rest of your life." So be thoughtful about what you do with it.

Life's small changes have great importance. From them grow individual, family, even global transformation. For anyone about to embark on some new project there is a hesitation, perhaps a fear. But without a good idea and adequate preparation, the new structure will never get built. Without a suitable training program, the marathon cannot be run. Without keying in sentence one, the book will never be written. Once we get things started, the new undertaking seems only half as daunting as our fears. Soon routine helps us continue, and before we know it we are halfway to our goal. Per the Chinese saying, the thousand-mile journey begins with that first step.

Proverbs in many languages underscore the importance, and the difficulty, of beginnings: "A good start is half the work" (Gaelic). "A good beginning makes a good end" (English). "Every beginning is hard" (German, Chinese, and other languages). So why not embrace the Nike slogan and "Just do it"?

Shall we begin?

For the first entry in your Wisdom Journal (hereafter WJ), write about some small choice you made that has had a major impact on your life. Happy journaling!

Active-Learning Wisdom

Tell me, and I'll forget. Show me, and I may not remember. Involve me, and I'll understand.

— A Native American Saying

What do you remember from school? For my part, I don't remember much. I obviously learned to read, write, and calculate. School and college learning in my day was primarily a spectator sport. The teacher lectured. We listened and took notes. Exceptions were science classes where we had occasional labs; or English and social studies, where we wrote papers. But the concept was, the teacher explained; the student listened and learned.

Learning by doing was the domain of sports, scouts, social life, summer camps, arts activities, and clubs. Here we didn't have teachers but coaches, scoutmasters, counselors, sponsors, tutors, and each other. We learned by participating. We also learned to get along with our peers, clean our plates, and be polite to our elders.

In life, we also learn by doing. Thanks to John Dewey and his ideas for progressive education, this natural strategy is now used in many schools and colleges. Computer technology helps students learn on their own through hundreds of interactive multimedia curricula. Service learning where students assist in community projects or at charities is common; and apprenticeship programs can be found around the country. A NASA satellite tracked by math and science students gives them a new way to acquire knowledge and techniques in their fields. As a teacher I believe telling and showing have their place as educational strategies. But as the saying reminds us, experience is still the best teacher.

Pick three of your important skills and describe in your WJ how you acquired them.

Aloha Wisdom

If you examine the history of the Hawaiian conversion to Christianity... they kept hold of their own traditions... [while] accepting other ways of life. [They had a] philosophical understanding that [all] humans are the same... This is the major contribution that Hawaiian spirituality has to make to the world's future.

– Rubellite Kawena Johnson, *Local Knowledge,*
Ancient Wisdom, 1991

The spirit of *aloha* (love, affection, compassion, mercy) impacts everyday life in Hawaii. On a mundane level, strangers smile at one another on the sidewalk, in the mall, and at the beach. Drivers seldom honk their horns but let others in with a friendly wave. You even call bus drivers "uncle" or "aunty."

More significantly, ethnic and racial intermarriage is the rule— nearly 50 percent of 50th-State marriages are mixed. Is the Old Adam still alive and well in Hawaii? Of course. It's a place filled with human beings. And yet...

In his two terms, our recent Honolulu-born President, Barack Obama, showed the Aloha Spirit in his low-key smiling personality, the way he played with kids or shot hoops, and his no-drama approach to both domestic and world affairs. His years in Indonesia, Chicago, and Boston doubtless also played a part in shaping the person he became. But his growing up in the Makiki District of Honolulu was clearly formative, as any long-time Hawaii resident would see and confirm.

When it comes to race and just plain human relations, Hawaii's tradition of aloha has a lot to teach the world.

In your WJ suggest three ways you might practice aloha wherever you live.

Arboreal Wisdom

I think that I shall never see,
A poem lovely as a tree
A tree that looks at God all day,
And lifts her leafy arms to pray...

– Joyce Kilmer (1886–1918), "Trees"

Kilmer's poem is considered a poster child for bad, sentimental poetry. How could I not agree? Still, the point on which it's based is well-taken and important.

Arbor is the Latin word for tree, the modern tradition of Arbor Day having begun in the 17th century. And I'll admit it—I am a tree hugger. What I experience from hugging trees is a sense of their strength and rectitude, qualities they seem willing to share with me.

Trees instinctively grow toward the sky. They have long lives and the resilience to stand their ground through all kinds of weather. Deep roots surely have something to do with it. They also offer shade to the earth and its creatures, provide homes to arboreal animals, and offer beauty to those who can perceive it. Moreover, they do all this in silence, without any request for payment or even gratitude.

Once I asked my inner self to help me understand what it means to be of service. I visualized a field full of trees breathing in carbon dioxide and exhaling the oxygen needed by us mammals. Maybe my feeling for trees is ancestral. After all, it was my people who thought up the Tree of Knowledge and the Tree of Life.

Write in your WJ about how you feel toward trees. Do they offer any lessons for your life? If possible, hug a tree and then write about your experience.

Aristotelian Wisdom

The wise man ought to know not only what follows from his first principles; he should know also the truth about these principles. Wisdom therefore will be a union of intuitive reason and scientific knowledge; it may be defined as the complete science of the loftiest matters.

— Aristotle (384–322 BCE), *Nicomachean Ethics*

The ancient Greeks gave the world both the terms and concepts *philosophy* and *philosopher*. They mean "love of wisdom" and "lover of wisdom," respectively. Plato and his student Aristotle are considered the fathers of Western philosophy.

To be sure, Plato and Aristotle loved wisdom in different ways. Of the two, Plato was the more mystical and poetic, Aristotle the more rational and scientific. Using contemporary terminology, we might call Plato a philosopher of the right brain, Aristotle a philosopher of the left.

Plato said, "Wise men speak because they have something to say; fools because they have to say something." For Aristotle, the wise person is not so much a sage who has learned to live the best possible life, but a logician who both knows first principles and can accurately derive what follows from these principles. One thinks of someone like Albert Einstein.

Aristotle also helped us understand the wisdom of the middle way. Courage, he explained, lies midway between foolhardiness (too much of it) and cowardice (too little).

Elsewhere, to be fair, Aristotle states, "Our idea of the truly good and wise man [sic] is that he bears all the changes of life with dignity and always does what is best in the circumstances." The middle way? Hopefully so.

In your WJ try writing your own definition of wisdom.

9

Asian Wisdom

We of the West still hold instinctively to the prejudice that our world and our civilization are the "whole world." ... But times are changing... It is vitally necessary for the West to understand the traditional thought of the great Asian cultures: China, India, and Japan. This is necessary not only for specialists, but for every educated person in the West.

– Thomas Merton (1915–1968)

Father Merton is one of the prophets of the 1960s. It took courage for him, a Trappist monk and ordained Catholic priest, to publish thoughts like these at a time when cultural and religious chauvinism were still in the ascendant. Not that intellectual and spiritual provincialism is dead, but at least many religious leaders now agree with Merton and echo his position.

Consider this statement by Pope John Paul II to a Japanese audience in 1981 when speaking in Tokyo: "You are the heirs and keepers of an ancient wisdom. This wisdom in Japan and the Orient has inspired high degrees of moral life. It has taught you to venerate the pure, transparent, and honest heart. It has inspired you to discover the divine presence in every creature, and especially in the human being."

As practitioners of a religion some not only consider best but feel called to spread to all humankind, we are well advised to refrain from proselytizing. Instead, we should learn from those different from us. Who knows how we might grow if we could hear the secrets the Universe may have whispered to others.

In your WJ discuss which non-Western influences have meant the most to you personally.

Authentic-Living Wisdom

Too many of us spend time doing things for… no heartfelt reason…
We do it to make a living, to satisfy the expectations of others…
but not because the doing comes from inside us. When our action is
dictated by factors external to our souls, we do not live active lives
but reactive lives.

— Parker J. Palmer, *The Active Life*, 1991

To follow educator Parker Palmer's sage advice, we have to be or become sensitive to who we are, what we are good at, and what makes our hearts sing. Then we have to have the courage of our convictions. If we are not careful, we can spend our lives doing things we don't like in order to maintain a lifestyle we do.

Back in the Sixties we encouraged each other to do our own thing. But how do we figure out what our own thing is? Or what happens when we are good at several things? In short, how do we identify our true talents and then determine how to use them in a way that will assure that we can support ourselves and our families?

Given this conundrum, our daily prayer might be the following: "O God, please help me be the self you have designed for me and grant me the strength to become that self fully. And please, if possible, let me earn my living in ways that enhance rather than deplete my soul while benefiting others. Amen."

In your WJ write about your work. If you're not doing so now, what changes must you make to really do your own thing?

Back-to-Basics Wisdom

May you have warmth in your igloo, oil in your lamp, and peace in your heart.

– An Eskimo Proverb

We don't need very much really. Shelter, light, and peace—and others or another to share them with. Many of us have lost our regard for the simple but important things of life. Growing older fortunately helps restore this appreciation. As our bodies begin to function less smoothly or well, we become grateful for each good night's sleep, well-digested meal, or pain-free day.

Life can be cold and hard. Having a place of our own that is not only physically but psychologically comforting—a home, not just a house or an apartment—is a great blessing. Being able to return to this nest for rest and recovery after a day's work or activities makes going out the next day possible.

To have the necessary provisions—oil in our lamps—is a blessing too. Not to be in want and thus in the dark is very important for living.

Most important, to be sure, is peace in our hearts. Being competitive, winning, or insisting on being right seems less appropriate as we age. Serenity comes to replace the winner's circle in the scheme of things. Give-and-take, especially with family and friends, comes to have a higher priority than winning. Letting go of that old imperative makes it easier for others to live with us and for us to live with ourselves. The basic of basics is realizing that the source of peace lies within.

What basics would you like to get back to in your life? Write briefly on this topic in your WJ.

Balanced Wisdom

To those who choose the path that leads to Enlightenment, there are two extremes that should be carefully avoided... indulgence in the desires of the body... [and]... ascetic discipline, torturing one's body and mind unreasonably.

– The Teaching of Buddha, Bukkyo Dendo Kyokai Edition

My late mother, who lived to be ninety-five, must have been a secret Buddhist. She always counseled me, with moderate success, to take it easy.

During my student year in Germany I read a history of ancient Greece, whose citizens made the Golden Mean their ideal precisely because of their tendency to be immoderate. Chinese medicine is based on a similar concept. Yin and Yang, those complementary forces of the universe, must remain in dynamic balance.

Aristotle's ethics is also based on the middle way. The classic example is courage, which for him fell midway between its own excess and deficiency. If you have too much, you'll be foolhardy; too little, a coward.

Come to think of it, the wisdom of the middle way is instilled into us as children by the story of Goldilocks, who tried out the three bears' chairs, beds, and food until she decided what was "just right" for her. We learn from childhood on to look for situations, friends, partners, and work that are "just right" —usually occurring somewhere between the extremes.

Much of the world's religious history is based on spiritual development through extreme practices. Fortunately, the Buddha brought a measure of moderation to spiritual training.

How balanced is your life? Write briefly in your WJ about how well you adhere to the middle way.

Best-Practice Wisdom

Alone we can do so little; together we can do so much.
— Helen Keller (1880–1968)

I first encountered the concept of best practices at 18. An exchange student in Germany, I was brought up short by the showers and the TV there. Back in 1958, the shower heads I knew in America were all fixed, whereas in Germany I experienced the removable ones you could take out of their holders and rinse yourself off at close range.

As for the TV, the quality of the picture, with greater resolution, was crisper than the grainy ones we still had—apparently thanks to a later, better patent. Some years on, the same proved true of their color TV images, which looked like Technicolor while ours still had people with green faces. And here I'd thought America had the best of everything!

Fifty-eight years later, filmmaker Michael Moore made the same point in his outstanding two-hour documentary, *Where to Invade Next?* In it Moore travels to a number of mainly European countries where he is blown away by things like eight weeks of paid vacation in Italy, quasi-gourmet meals in French elementary schools, free university education even for foreigners in Slovenia, government-paid spa visits for health in Germany, humane prisons in Norway, and required gender-balance on corporate boards in Iceland. This was the booty he wanted to bring home to the USA.

Why can we get Swedish furniture and Thai food here while refusing to adopt outstanding public policies from abroad? National arrogance can really keep countries from being truly great.

Write in your WJ about some international practice you'd like implemented in your country.

Bright-Star Wisdom

In the December of your life, you have two
responsibilities: to prepare for your own death
and to bless those coming after you.
   – Paraphrased from Sara Davidson's *The December Project*
   (2014) about Rabbi Zalman Schachter-Shalomi (1924–2014)

I was fortunate to have attended Reb Zalman's last public appearance. A Hassidic rabbi, he was in dialogue with his then most-recent biographer, Sara Davidson, at not a local synagogue in his hometown, Boulder, Colorado, but the First Congregational Church. That was Reb Zalman.

When I described this standing-room-only event to my wife, who had been out of town, we began thinking about how we two septuagenarians might respond to his second recommendation, possibly as a way of achieving the first. What we came up with was Bright Stars.

For four years we have met once a month with a group of young women ages 23 to 38. Of the 30 or so on our roster, only two are married. Most have college or advanced degrees. Several are from abroad and a few are of color. On a given Friday evening seven to 12 will show up for a potluck at our house to interact for a few hours with a visiting mentor, mainly an accomplished older woman who shares her life and wisdom with them.

The visiting mentors go away with their faith in the younger generation strengthened, while the Bright Stars are enthusiastic about what they've heard. Meanwhile, the Stars have become a little community and have formed new friendships. It's been a rich experience for all of us.

Write for five minutes in your WJ about how you might "bless those
coming after you."

Charismatic Wisdom

God is always present. The question is,
how present are we?
– Zalman Schachter-Shalomi (1924–2014), *Davening: A Guide to*
Meaningful Jewish Prayer, 2012

My first encounter with Reb Zalman was in spring of 1957. I was a 17-year-old Yale freshman. He was a 32-year-old Jewish chaplain at the University of Manitoba, in Winnipeg, Canada. The context was the Friday evening Shabbat service.

Rabbi Israel, our Hillel chaplain, was dressed in preppy tweeds, as we all were, the unofficial dress code back then for Ivy Leaguers. Reb Zalman, a Lubavitcher Hassid, clearly marched to a different drummer.

He was arrayed—the only word for it—in tall black boots, an ermine-trimmed cloak, a big black belt, and a fur hat. A large man with a European accent, he commanded the space with his impressive charisma. I could read the thoughts of my fellow Jewish Yalies: "Who is this bozo?" Five minutes later, he had us all dancing in the aisles as we intoned with him the melodies of Jewish *nigunim*, traditional songs without words.

Reb Zalman later created the organization for Spiritual Eldering, wrote *From Age-ing to Sage-ing*, founded the ecumenical Jewish Renewal movement, was the first World Wisdom chairholder at Boulder's Buddhist university (Naropa), wrote several other books on Jewish and spiritual subjects, hung out with the Dalai Lama, and, along the way, dropped acid with Timothy Leary; did Zen, Subud, and a number of other spiritual practices; trained a host of distinguished rabbis; and died just short of 90, beloved by both Jews and non-Jews alike.

Who is the most charismatic person you know? Write in your WJ about
her or him.

Children's Wisdom

Dear God,
What does it mean you are a jealous God?
I thought you had everything.
Jane

> – From Stuart Hample and Eric Marshall, *Children's*
> *Letters to God*, 1966

If the world's classical traditions attribute wisdom to age, the romantics saw it in children. It took the boy in Hans Christian Andersen's *The Emperor's New Clothes* to see—and say—the emperor was naked.

Yet the innocent eye does not merely fade with time. It is educated out of us. Some of us elders may remember Lieutenant Cable's song in *South Pacific*. In love with a young Polynesian woman on the island where he is stationed, Cable knows he will never be able to marry and take her back to the States. So, he sings about the need to be taught in the early years, before it's too late, to "hate all the people his relatives hate." Being carefully taught in this way becomes the basis for our prejudices.

So, Jane writes God and challenges Exodus 20:5, "For I the LORD thy God am a jealous God" (KJV). To Jane, *jealous* means *envious*. She remembers her friend Sally taunting her, "Janie, you're just jealous because my doll's prettier." Jane reasons, "Why should God be jealous when God already has everything?"

It often takes the fresh mind of a child to see through the contradictions of society. We should thus remember Jesus' advice that unless we become like little children, we will never enter the Kingdom of heaven.

Can you remember something you knew or said as a child that was
"beyond your years"? In your WJ write about this experience of childhood
wisdom.

Classroom Wisdom

And this our life, exempt from public haunt, finds tongues in trees, books in the running brooks, sermons in stones and good in everything.
– William Shakespeare (1564–1616), *As You Like It*, II.1.15–17

In Spring 1990 I began planning a course called "The Literature of Wisdom." It was to be about increasing one's personal wisdom. By the time I'd moved to Hawaii in fall, 1996, it had been offered to full classrooms twelve times.

Class met one night per week for three hours over fourteen weeks. The first session consisted of self-introductions, individual definitions of wisdom, and a course orientation. The last class was a potluck party at my house where we read our finals aloud—letters to our fellow class participants. The questions never changed: (1) What are three things I got out of this course? (2) What do I think wisdom is now? (3) What am I sure it is not? (4) What are three things I intend to do now to become wiser? and (5) What final thoughts can I share?

In the closing circle there were always some tears. We had looked at a variety of works, from ancient to modern, literary to popular. The second session was always on proverbial wisdom. A popular assignment was to write a one-page letter giving someone else advice for living "the good life." Everyone also did a class journal and final group project. What impressed me was how much natural wisdom we each had. Learning wisdom together in a safe environment, we forged a powerful sense of community. We had come home.

In your WJ reflect on how you might live more wisely.

Community Wisdom

The only answer to this life, to the loneliness we are all bound to feel, is community[:] ... the living together, working together, sharing together, loving God and loving our brother, and living close to him in community so we can show our love for Him.
– Dorothy Day (1897–1980), *The Long Loneliness*

Dorothy Day was an American journalist and social activist. Her first job in the early 1920s was as a reporter with the *New York Call*, a socialist newspaper. There she participated in protests leading to time in jail.

In 1933, after converting to Catholicism, Dorothy met Peter Maurin, a Catholic social reformer from France. They cofounded the *Catholic Worker*, a newspaper for which Dorothy continued to write and serve as editor until her death 47 years later. She reached out to the poor, protested unfair labor practices, emphasized the importance of living close to the land, and practiced pacifism. Today the *Catholic Worker* is still in print, and 245 Catholic Worker communities offer shelter, food, and social services to poor and homeless people of all backgrounds worldwide.

Dorothy believed in the "brotherhood" of extended families. Through the parenthood of God, all human beings, she felt, were brothers and sisters and should act accordingly. To avoid what she referred to in her autobiography as "the long loneliness," we should band together in effective communities, where the whole is greater and more impactful than the sum of its parts. But that may beg the question of where the individual stops and the collective begins.

How do you balance personal development and social reform in your life? Respond in your WJ.

Computer Wisdom

Bill Moyers: What about the argument that machines, like computers, dehumanize learning?
Isaac Asimov: As a matter of fact, it's just the reverse… Everyone can have a teacher in the form of access to the gathered knowledge of the human species.

— Bill Moyers, *A World of Ideas*, 1989

One of my former bosses didn't own a computer. He even eschewed electric typewriters, preferring to draft memos on an old manual from his reporting days. I used to feel the same way. I insisted on doing my creative writing in pen on a legal pad. I believed inspiration would flow more freely that way. Once I became aware of such computer benefits as cutting and pasting, copying, and word counting, however, I changed my tune.

The late Isaac Asimov, to be sure, was not talking about word processing. A true futurist, he saw — well before the Internet revolution — how computers could make the world's knowledge available to virtually everyone.

Information technology, moreover, is perhaps one of the few areas in society, along with e-car batteries, where power and sophistication rise while prices fall. Thanks to the brilliance of Apple founder Steve Jobs and others, increasing numbers can now buy a tablet or smartphone and have the world at their fingertips. Google, Wikipedia, and TEDTalks are cost-free educational magic carpets.

Computer technology and its first cousin, artificial intelligence, are not without problems. But it is wise to remember the potential while working to shape the best possible reality.

Discuss in your WJ the benefits and drawbacks of online learning. How would you assure that computers and A.I. work for, not against, us?

Confucian Wisdom

By three methods we may learn wisdom: First, by reflection, which is noblest; second, by imitation, which is easiest; and third, by experience, which is bitterest.

— Confucius (551–479 BCE), *Analects*, Translated by Arthur Waley

Confucius, like many Chinese throughout history, spoke in proverbs. Slogans of the People's Republic of China are also proverbial in form. One I learned in Chinese class—"Friendship first, competition second!" [*Youyi di yi, bisai di er!*]—would be ritually intoned before sports matches, whereupon each team would do its best to smash its opponent.

Much of Confucian wisdom is based on the distinction between how a magnanimous person and a small-minded person would act in various situations. Each proverbial statement set up a clear contrast between the right way and the wrong way to behave. For example, the magnanimous person follows the law while the small-minded person looks for ways around it. The magnanimous individual considers whether something is right; the small-minded person asks if it will pay. The big-hearted human being under-promises and over-delivers, while the small-minded person does just the opposite. Confucius has many other similar statements.

Limited understanding leads to or reinforces narrow-mindedness which in turn fosters selfish, shortsighted, even criminal behavior. As you see things, so you act.

Generous vision, generous heart, generous action: These are the characteristics of Confucius' ideal person and are not far removed from those of the nineteenth-century's "Christian gentleman," the masculinist term for today's noble human being. Confucian wisdom nevertheless still applies to our life today.

In which areas are you broad-minded? In which, less so? How might you become more magnanimous? Discuss these questions in your WJ.

Conversing-with-God Wisdom

God is speaking to all of us, all the time. The question is not, to whom does God talk? The question is, who listens?

– Neale Donald Walsch

I'll admit I talk with God regularly. While I don't actually hear someone speaking, I always feel a Presence inside and am convinced that my inner calls are being answered. Before hanging up, I'm quietly confident about having gotten guidance for my questions and knowing what to do next.

I first heard the voice of an older man talking to me from inside when I was six. My mother had just tucked me in and prayed the *Now I Lay Me Down to Sleep* prayer with me. She then turned off the light and left the room. Suddenly the "if I should die before I wake" line came back to me, and I was terrified. "God, I'm too young to die, only six. I haven't done anything yet. Please let me live!"

Then that voice told me that no one is too young to die. Still, I shouldn't worry. I would live to be an old man and mentioned what sounded like a pretty big number to me at the time. Comforted, I fell asleep and wasn't scared by my mother's prayer anymore.

I also felt reassured when Neale Donald Walsch began writing his *Conversations with God* books. We all talk to God whenever we pray. And God speaks to us too, but in order to hear, we have to learn to listen. Meantime, in my calls to God, I hope I'm becoming a better listener.

In your WJ describe how you communicate with God.

Decisive Wisdom

Once you make a decision, the universe conspires to make it happen.
– Ralph Waldo Emerson (1803–1882)

We all know the limitations of this wisdom. The universe will not help me if I decide to fly, arms flapping, off the Empire State Building. But we also instinctively know what Emerson is saying. If we put all our energy into something—really go for it—we do start to see things breaking our way. It's almost as if the universe respects our spunk and decides to help out.

Even failure becomes grist for our mill. A friend of mine in Chicago, a poet, started his career teaching difficult children in a home for boys. Someone suggested that he might like to join him in buying a cassette-duplicating business. My friend took the plunge, and it became a long, hard fall. After years of effort, he declared bankruptcy.

Meanwhile he had learned many new skills and became adept at raising money. When he bought into an existing software company, again there were challenges. But before long he produced a successful data-management program, and his picture one day appeared on the cover of a software magazine. A few years later his company was bought out by Apple. He must have done very well, because he was able to make a seven-figure donation to charity.

I have noticed in my own life that when I make a major decision and persevere, things do fall into place. It's not easy being decisive, but the universe seems clearly to reward this kind of behavior.

In your WJ comment on whether and how Emerson's claim has manifested in your life.

Deferred-Gratification Wisdom

Manage with bread and salted butter until Allah brings something to eat with them.

– A Moroccan Proverb

My friend Binh was a boat person who left Vietnam with nothing but the clothes on his back and a wristwatch. After months in a Thai refugee camp, an international organization secured his release and flew him to Vienna, where he began learning German and working as a draftsman in an architectural firm.

I met Binh in Chicago soon after he joined his parents and seven siblings there. His father and mother had menial jobs, but the children were brilliant in school—several attending college, some taking part-time jobs. The family lived together in a cramped apartment, pooling all their money, never complaining. Within a few years Binh, now an architect, moved up at a large architectural firm, and the children were soon collectively earning enough so that the parents could retire.

I once asked Binh when he planned to marry (he was in his forties). "Not yet," he replied. As the oldest responsible male after his father, he needed to wait until his last sibling had completed college. I understood: that was how it was in his Confucian culture. Before long, however, he married; then in short order several sons arrived.

Binh and his family personified the saying, "All things come to those who wait"—and work hard. By deferring gratification, all the family members were eventually doing well. It was an international success story: The American dream done Vietnamese-style, bearing out the truth of the Moroccan proverb.

Are you willing to defer gratification for a goal you have? Explore this concept in your WJ.

Divine Wisdom

Wisdom is the principal thing; therefore, get wisdom.
                                          – Proverbs 4:7 (KJV)

"Can people *become* wiser?" This is a question I frequently get when individuals find out I have written a number of books about wisdom and am intent on raising the world's wisdom quotient. Their question implies that wisdom is inherited, like blue eyes or brown hair, or if they are religious, that it's a special charism, or gift, from God. Sometimes my questioners admit to harboring the belief that wisdom was limited to ancient times. Back in the days of Socrates and Jesus there were reportedly miracles and sages. Nowadays we have science and charlatans. Wise guys you can find in abundance, they declare. But as for the truly wise, forget it! That was then; this is now.

What about us garden-variety middle-class, college-educated Westerners? We can become more credentialed, better skilled in a specialty, more highly paid for our work, more respected by our colleagues. But wiser?

A second quotation from Proverbs (2:6), *"The Lord giveth wisdom,"* is a source of both hope and despair. Jesus' A.S.K. formula is a central tenet of his ministry: Ask, and what you request will be given. Seek, and what you need will be found. Knock, and the door to what you desire will be opened from the inside. It seems that the Universe has provided us with everything we require to become wiser *if* we simply believe and make an effort to find it. Yet getting from here to there is likely an uphill slog.

Do you think people can become wiser? Are you becoming wiser? Respond to these questions in your WJ.

Do-Over Wisdom

If at first you don't succeed, try, try again.

— An American saying

My wife is a psychotherapist who comes from the most functional family I've ever met. I mean, they really get along, decide things together, and harmony prevails.

So, in the nine years Cedar and I have been together, I've learned a lot from her about maintaining and strengthening good relations. Not that my family of origin was dysfunctional. In fact, the older I get, the more decent and loving it has come to seem. Still, if the Barstows of Wethersfield, Connecticut, were major-league winners, the Feldmans of Manhattan, New York, were only little-league champs.

In this regard, one of the best things I've learned from Cedar has been the technique of the do-over. When my critical Scorpio nature gets the better of me, I will say something hurtful. It's true that if the backdoor is left open, flying critters will enter the house. Still, it is unnecessary for me to say something thoughtless like, "Can't you see how your carelessness has invited in all the flies and bees in the neighborhood. Can't you be more considerate?!"

She'll respond with, "You're right, but the way you put that hurt my feelings. Can we try a do-over?" I get it, apologize, and will say something softer like, "Dear, can we both try to keep the backdoor closed to keep the flies out?" "Sure," she'll say. "I'm sorry I left it open." We then hug, the negativity resolved, and our relationship is strengthened.

Write in your WJ about a technique you use to maintain or enhance good relations with someone close to you.

Earth Wisdom

I do not see a delegation
For the Four-Footed.
I see no seat for the eagles.
We forget and we consider
Ourselves superior...
And we stand somewhere between
The mountain and the Ant.
Somewhere and only there
As part and parcel
Of the Creation.

– Chief Oren Lyons, "Consciousness"

For a few years I worked in and around American Indian country. I evaluated grant requests on reservations or at tribally controlled colleges and raised funds for school curricula Buffy Sainte-Marie developed "through Native American eyes." I came to respect the Natives' cultural connections with Mother Earth.

My first encounter with an indigenous person occurred in 1991. That summer I spent a weekend at a small conference with Chief Oren Lyons, spokesperson for the Six Nations Iroquois Confederacy. Oren had organized a loose association of the world's indigenous peoples, which he represented at the United Nations. Since the four-footed and the eagles couldn't argue their own needs, he endeavored to do so for them. He spoke quietly but with passion. His points were difficult to refute.

Earth wisdom begins with realizing that we humans are part of the natural world, not its owner. Lack of respect for our world has already resulted in the wholesale loss of plant and animal species and the degradation of air, land, and water. Native traditions emphasize living lightly on the Earth. Rather than trying to "civilize" the Native Americans and other primal peoples, we would do well to learn from them.

What do you do that has a positive impact on the natural world? How might you improve your practice? Write on this topic in your WJ.

Ecumenical Wisdom

In all of human history there has never been such an urgent need for ecumenical vitality... We live in a global village inhabited not only by Christians but by people of other nations, other religions, other cultures.

– Choan-Seng Song, President, World Alliance of Reformed Churches, 1997–2004

The fellowship Reverend Song, a Chinese American, presided over for seven years, in 2017 comprised more than seventy-five million Christians in over 100 countries. Two-thirds live in Africa, Asia, and Latin America. Given this diversity it is understandable that he expressed such inclusive views, despite the fact that his churches are successors to the intolerant Puritans of Colonial New England. Early Quakers, for example, risked life and limb to practice their beliefs in Massachusetts in the late seventeenth century and had to move to Roger Williams' more tolerant community in Rhode Island.

Long ago, when the world's population was smaller, scattered, and less mobile, most people lived amid others with similar appearances and beliefs. Inclusiveness was not an issue then. Natural disasters and political wars, however, caused wholesale movements of peoples. Today, willy-nilly, we live in a global village.

This village nevertheless has neighborhoods with ethnic hostilities and other challenges. It will take many more leaders like the Reverend Song to help us understand that we belong to one family, live on one planet, exist in one universe, and have been formed by one Creator. As residents of a single global village, we must find the wisdom to live together in harmony, creativity, and peace. Planetary survival requires it.

What does ecumenism mean to you? Write briefly on this topic in your WJ.

Editorial Wisdom

Even the best writer has to erase.

– A Spanish saying

Tell me about it! And I'm far from the best writer. At least the computer makes editing easy now. In the old days of cut-and-paste, we *really* had to cut and paste. We English majors at Yale were given so many writing assignments that writing and editing became a single late-night activity.

During the 1960s and 1970s, research in composition showed it advisable to separate writing from editing. Teachers would assign free-writing exercises, instructing their students to put down their thoughts as they came and not to worry about organization, grammar, punctuation, or spelling. Polishing could come later.

Research also showed that we write from the creative right side of the brain but edit from the logical left. Editors can be creative, but their job is to make improvements to what someone else has written. Mostly, though, we have to be our own editors. The best strategy is thus to put our work aside for a few days or even weeks before reviewing it. Then we can come to it as if someone else had written it. Even a few hours will give us some critical distance.

In the editing mode, we should try to place ourselves in the shoes of our readers. Will they understand what we are writing? Will they know the acronyms, the historical references? Is our vocabulary too technical, too simple? Are our sentences too long or short? This book is being edited by professionals, so here's hoping they have answered such questions to your satisfaction.

In your WJ discuss how you write and edit your own work.

Educational Wisdom

Educit obstetrix, educat nutrix...
(The midwife draws out, the wet nurse feeds.)
– Marcus Terentius Varro (116–27 BCE)

Education is perhaps the most misderived word in English. A year won't go by without my reading from a sincere author, even a classically trained German scholar, that the term comes from Latin and means "to draw out." The usual conclusion is that education is thus a process of drawing forth knowledge from the student.

Well, these authors get it partially right. Our term does come from Latin. The problem is that it derives from the first-conjugation verb *educare*, to feed, not the third-conjugation one, *educere*, to draw out. If the latter were the case, our term would be "eduction" (cp. "reduction," to lead back; "production," to lead forth; or "seduction," to lead away).

There are in fact two approaches to education, the classical and the romantic. The former ascribes to the idea that the teacher feeds, or fills, the otherwise ignorant pupil with knowledge. The latter is based on the belief that individuals are already endowed with what they need to know. Like ore, this innate intelligence only requires to be extracted and refined.

The truth doubtless lies somewhere in between. Like babies we need to be fed, but the principle of growth preexists within us. We can't learn to fly a plane or speak Portuguese by intuition. The requisite know-how comes from outside expertise. The motivation and necessary learning nevertheless rest with us. In education, then, both these activities are required. No wonder the *Encyclopaedia Britannica* calls Varro "Rome's greatest scholar."

In your WJ discuss your philosophy of education.

Enlightenment Wisdom

What is this light that shines through the chinks of my mind and pierces my heart, doing it no injury? ... Wisdom it is, none other than Wisdom, that shines through my darkness, tearing apart the cloud that envelopes me.

> – St. Augustine (354–430), *The Confessions*, Translated by Maria Boulding

The term *wisdom* when capitalized by Christian writers usually refers to an attribute of Christ. It is the light of God's grace that seeks us out, shines through our darkness, and, as Augustine puts it, tears apart the cloud that surrounds us. We can then see things clearly, in a new light.

Interestingly, some etymologists argue that *wisdom* and *vision* both derive from the same source, the past participle of the Latin verb "to see": *visus*. Thus wisdom would depend on our ability to see things clearly.

Another Christian view is that wisdom, like vision, is a charism, a divinely conferred gift. The Bible gives us a verse about the wisdom to know God: *"I pray that the God of our Lord Jesus Christ, the all-glorious Father, may give you the spiritual powers of wisdom and vision, by which there comes the knowledge of Him"* (Ephesians 1:17).

As for knowing God, can a table know the carpenter who made it? Still, as creatures endowed with consciousness, we may be able to experience God, to know the God within us. This has always been the premise of mystics, whose goal is union with the indwelling Divine. Let us pray that we each may be enlightened and come to know our Creator in this way.

Write in your WJ what enlightenment means to you.

Entrepreneurial Wisdom

If something's important enough, you should try. Even if the probable outcome is failure.
– Elon Musk on *60 Minutes*, March 30, 2014

Back in 2000, no one outside his family and friends had heard of Elon Musk. Now, 18 years later, with an estimated net worth of $15.2 billion dollars, he is the 80th wealthiest person on the planet. In December 2016, moreover, *Forbes* listed him as the 21st most powerful individual worldwide.

To name all the entrepreneurial projects he's been involved in would exceed the word limit of this essay. The South African kid who read through and memorized whole chunks of the *Encyclopaedia Britannica* has now put his creative genius to work on freeing the earth from its harmful dependence on fossil fuel. The results to date are Tesla, SolarCity, the Gigafactory, and SpaceX. Oh, and he launched himself by creating PayPal.

His all-electric cars, becoming increasingly affordable, have caused automakers around the world to start rushing their own battery-powered vehicles to market. China has just decided to phase out all traditional vehicles. Meantime, Tesla is among the most valuable car companies in the United States. SolarCity is the second largest installer of solar arrays in the country, and the Nevada-based Gigafactory will one day be turning out car and home-storage batteries in the largest factory in the world.

Elon has already launched the first rocket to successfully land on its tail for reuse. His big dream, though, is to create a viable earth colony on Mars by 2030, in case life on earth becomes impossible.

In your WJ write about an entrepreneurial individual you know.

Equal-Rights Wisdom

Our struggle today is not to have a female Einstein get appointed as an assistant professor. It is for a woman schlemiel to get as quickly promoted as a male schlemiel.

– Bella Abzug (1920–1998)

I was living in Chicago during the years when the Equal Rights Amendment failed to be ratified by the required two-thirds of the states. Illinois was among the holdouts. Consequently, many national conferences forsook Chicago and rebooked in pro-ERA states. The National Conference on Higher Education was one. I henceforth had to find the funds to fly to D.C. or San Francisco and stay at the conference hotel.

When I moved to Chicago in 1973 to direct program development at an innovative state university, I discovered the internal finalist for the job had been the women's studies coordinator. Members of that program had protested the naming of an outside male to the position. The situation was especially tricky since Women's Studies fell within my administrative responsibility. Fortunately, I was genuinely interested in furthering women's studies, and my unsuccessful rival proved a good sport. So things worked out, and we became supportive colleagues to one another.

Equal rights may be long in coming. With children of the same parents frequently unable to get along, how will strangers ever be able to collaborate and regard each other as members of a single harmonious family? There are so many areas of difference to overcome. When will all schlemiels be created equal and that amendment be passed? Still, despite emerging sexual predators, some progress has been made.

Discuss in your WJ your feelings and opinions about a Constitutional amendment on equal rights.

Eternal-Light Wisdom

In my grandfather's synagogue there was a light that never went out... It signifies that the unseen presence of God is always in this place.
— Rachel Naomi Remen, M.D., *Kitchen Table Wisdom*, 1996

According to my mother, the first word I said—probably after "Mama" and "Papa"—was "light." Apparently, I pointed to a lamp as I was saying it. And although I was a Hebrew-school dropout, I do remember a few words and phrases. One is *Nair Tamid*, "eternal light."

As I grew older, I discovered that light is a recurring theme in much spiritual and secular literature. The Judeo-Christian creation story is "God commanded: *Let there be light.*" In my twenties I heard a Hindu swami at the local Vedanta-Vivekananda temple intone, "Lead us from the darkness into the light." A few years later, while studying the Indonesian culture, I learned that the Javanese feminist Princess Kartini entitled her memoir *From Darkness into Light*. Later still, I gained a sense of the mystical meanings associated by Sufis with the term *noor*, *"light,"* the first cousin of the Hebrew *nair*.

In recent times Archbishop Desmond Tutu has said, "Hope is being able to see that there is light despite all of the darkness." This view may also be reflected by those who see a "figure of light" in near-death experiences, where the light is described as warm and welcoming. May our own journey from darkness lead us to the warm, welcoming eternal light of God. Meantime, let us work to bring more light into the world.

In your WJ write about the role of light in your life.

Experiential Wisdom

Histories make men wise.

– Francis Bacon (1561–1626)

Sir Francis Bacon was England's Renaissance man. He knew everything about everything and wrote essays on what he knew. Truth, death, revenge, adversity, marriage, the single life, atheism, travel, empire, fortune, law, boldness, vicissitude, and gardening are just a sampling of his topics. For individuals unable to believe that a commoner from the country could have written Shakespeare's plays, Bacon, the urbane aristocrat, has often been considered the genius behind the quill.

He was also the king of one-liners—short, pithy sentences which opened his essays. In "Of Gardens," for example, he begins, "God Almighty first planted a garden." Today's lead quotation begins a somewhat longer list of how different areas of study can impact us: "Histories make men wise; poets witty; the mathematics, subtle; natural philosophy, deep; moral [philosophy], grave; [and] logic and rhetoric, able to contend [that is, debate]."

Perhaps his major point about history, books, and wisdom is that we should learn from both the successes and mistakes of others. We can see the role of cause and effect in fictional characters' lives too. Early novels like *Moll Flanders* and *Tom Jones* were formally titled *The History of...* Most important, of course, is to profit from our own triumphs and setbacks, our own history. Experience after all is the best teacher. Of course, the learning is up to us. This maxim might help: "Don't live in the past or lament it. Learn from it." Or perhaps, "One-time mistakes are the best."

Discuss in your WJ an experience—a piece of your personal history— from which you gained some wisdom.

Exploratory Wisdom

Twenty years from now you will be more disappointed by the things that you didn't do than by the ones you did do. So throw off the bowlines. Sail away from the safe harbor. Catch the trade winds in your sails. Explore. Dream. Discover.

– Mark Twain (1835–1910)

Nowadays we encourage each other to "Go for it!" In the 1960s Ram Dass instructed, "Do it now!" For now, as Eastern traditions caution, is the only time we have for sure. Say "I'm sorry" and "I love you" *now*. Handle that difficult family or business situation *now*. Later may be too late. There may be no later.

Twain's advice is not just about personal initiatives. It could be the credo of everyone leaving the safety of accepted truth and striking out for undiscovered countries of the mind. Take Galileo, asserting that the earth circled the sun against the accepted opinion of his day. Trouble with his church resulted. If Aristotle and the church fathers believed that all heavenly bodies circled the earth, who was Galileo to assert otherwise?

Lord Tennyson (1809–1892) may have been the source of Twain's sailing metaphor. In "Ulysses" he draws on the legend that Odysseus was the first explorer to search out the Western Atlantic:

... Come, my friends,
'Tis not too late to seek a newer world.
... For my purpose holds
To sail beyond the sunset, and the paths
Of all the western stars, until I die.

Like Ulysses, let's sail beyond the sunset to seek our newest worlds.

Write in your WJ about your willingness to shed old views and explore new ones.

Family Wisdom

The family is the nucleus of civilization.
— Will Durant (1885–1981)

I believe in the wisdom of both the small family and the big one, the smallest and largest concepts of home.

In my family, "Are they Jewish?" was a fundamental question, especially for my Grandma Ida, the daughter of a scribe who meticulously copied Torah scrolls at the rate of one or two per year. She believed that humanity began and ended with the descendants of Abraham, Isaac and Jacob. Both my grandfathers took another stance by socializing with Gentiles. My mother's father, a farmer in southern New Jersey after the rigors of Ellis Island, came to be known by his Jewish neighbors as "goyischer Max" ("Gentile Max").

I grew up in a different world: An African-American housekeeper who was my surrogate mother, a Baptist boarding school, Yale, my junior year in Germany, a German Gentile wife, employment at the East-West Center in Hawaii, friendships with Catholic nuns and priests. I adopted the concepts of *tiospaye* from the Lakota and *ohana* from the Hawaiians, both terms meaning "extended kin group."

While we can't choose our biological family, we have the opportunity to go beyond this apparent limitation and expand the concept to include those people who have become the relatives of our heart. The world's people can be our sisters and brothers. The practice of marriage actually symbolizes the fact of a stranger growing into our closest family. In this way we can trade in our tribal passport for global citizenship.

What is your notion of family? What wisdom have you gained from family life? Discuss these concepts in your WJ.

Fearless Wisdom

The world is a very narrow bridge. The main thing is not to be afraid.
– As quoted from a Hasidic rabbi by Ellen Kushner on
WGBH's *Sound & Spirit*

The first thing biblical angels say to earthlings is "Fear Not!" I wonder how aliens, if they exist, greet humans? Creatures from out of this world, whether spiritual or material, are by definition scary.

Life itself is. Just getting up each day can be challenging. Will I be able to finish everything on my "to do" list? Will I be able to deal with what comes up? Will I die?

Let's follow the image of the world as a narrow wooden bridge—shaky, strung between two unequal cliffs, with a sheer drop of a thousand feet between them. Yet once here we have little choice but to cross. Consequently, one of the greatest spiritual gifts, according to the Vietnamese Buddhist monk Thich Nhat Hanh, is the state of no-fear. The fruit of inner development, we have to work hard to attain it. But once gained, we can do what's needed in our life in this world.

Fear's close relative is worry. Learning to live one day at a time, focusing on the here and now, is an excellent practice to keep one's worry-ometer low. The main thing is to be in relationship with one's Higher Power. For if we know that the Universe has our back, even the valley of the shadow of death won't keep us from crossing the world's narrow bridge.

How close are you to freedom from fear? Write in your WJ what steps you might take to get closer.

Feeling-Alive Wisdom

What we're all seeking is a meaning for life... an experience of being alive, so that our life... on the purely physical plane will have resonance within our innermost being and reality, so that we actually feel the rapture of being alive.
    – Joseph Campbell (1904–1987), *The Power of Myth*, 1988

In our materialistic civilization we learn to take actions to help us acquire things. Put another way, we know so we can do so we can have. An ironic bumper sticker in vogue some years ago called these false values to our attention: "Whoever dies with the most toys wins." There is a similar thought in Jesus' question, "For what is the value to people if they gain the whole world at the cost of their souls?" (Matthew 16:26).

Fortunately, we are so made that most of us are never satisfied with material things alone. Sometimes, though, we chase the pot of gold at the end of the rainbow, but the rainbow keeps eluding us until it disappears. We are truly fortunate, then, when we come to understand that material possessions are just not the golden road to happiness.

But if not possessions, what? Then we find another, more solid goal: the meaning of life. That gets us closer to Joseph Campbell's point. He counsels us to follow our bliss. Feeling happy will indicate when we have struck gold in a relationship, our profession, or living. The proper progression, Campbell implies, is to know in order to become in order to be.

In your WJ describe an experience when you felt "the rapture of being alive."

Gender Wisdom

The Wild Man is part of a company... in a man's psyche [as is] the Warrior... The Wild Man lives in complicated interchanges with the other interior beings. A whole community of beings is what is called a grown man.

– Robert Bly, *Iron John*, 1990

Our Creator has put into us the seeds of our own development, both individually and as a species. Life itself contains this force, called evolution. The last few hundred years have seen a number of major movements. The industrial, atomic, technological, and genetic revolutions, among them. The antislavery, pro-labor, civil and human-rights, and pro-democracy movements are some others. More recently, the women's movement has inspired a men's movement. Both have spiritual as well as political ramifications.

I am widely read in women's studies and believe there are important differences between the genders. To become whole, men need to recognize and draw on their feminine side, while women need to do the same with their masculine side.

According to Confucius, "Wisdom, compassion, and courage are the three universally recognized moral qualities of humans." Men need to come to terms with what makes them men by balancing their Warrior and Wild Man with their "other interior beings," as Bly states. I find this balance via membership in three men's groups, a male-only meditation group, and the co-ed Intentional Community at church. Gender wisdom for me means identifying and nurturing the masculine within us if we are women or the feminine within us if we are men while giving due consideration to the rest.

Discuss in your WJ what your gender means to you.

Getting-It Wisdom

A word to the wise is sufficient.

– An English Saying

It took me a while to get what these seven words meant. Finally, one day I got it. I don't remember doing anything different. In some mysterious way, between one hearing and the next, what had always before been opaque became transparent. I was blind but now I saw.

"Getting it" happens in all kinds of endeavors, not just with words. We remember the miracles of learning to float, then to swim. Or of riding a bicycle for the first time. We fail and fail and fail. Then, miraculously, we get it. And the nicest part is, once we get it, we never for-get it.

Imagine my delight when I *got*, from reading one of Ralph Waldo Emerson's essays, that *seer* is really *see-er*. Elsewhere I learned, with similar joy, that *atonement* derives from *at-onement*; that *enthusiasm* comes from God (Greek *theos*) being in us; that *inspiration* means having the *spirit within*; and that *insight* implies *seeing* into something, not simply taking it at face value.

The same holds not just for knowledge but for correction and judgment. You don't need to say much to a wise person who makes a mistake. They usually acknowledge the error right away and are capable of avoiding the same mistake in the future.

I think when we suddenly *get* something, God is in us. We are at one with what we get—*inspired, enthused*. We were blind but now we see. Enough said! I'm sure we've all gotten my drift by now.

Recall an instance of "getting" something. Write about the experience in your WJ.

Global-Village Wisdom

We are all astronauts on a little spaceship called Earth.
— Buckminster Fuller (1895–1983)

In the 1960s architect and inventor "Bucky" Fuller talked about *Spaceship Earth* as a self-sufficient vehicle riding around the solar system. It would be able to support its passengers in perpetuity so long as they did not overtax its carrying capacity through population increase or poor management. He felt we needed to know how to live together peacefully and effectively and to that end wrote his *Operating Manual for Spaceship Earth* (1968).

As the new millennium dawned, one could find the following online: If we could shrink the earth's population to a village of precisely 100 people, with all the existing human ratios remaining the same, there would be 57 Asians, 21 Europeans, 14 from the Western Hemisphere, 8 Africans; 52 females, 48 males; 70 nonwhites and non-Christians, 30 whites and Christians; 89 heterosexuals, 11 homosexuals. Fifty-nine percent of the world's wealth would be in the hands of only six people—all U.S. citizens. Eighty would live in substandard housing; 70 would be unable to read; and 50 would suffer from malnutrition. One would have a college education; one would own a computer.

These inequities will likely destabilize global society as the world shrinks. When considering the planet from such a compressed perspective, the need for acceptance, understanding, and cooperation becomes apparent. Wisdom suggests that prevention is the best cure, and the sooner we help one another achieve inner and outer sufficiency, the better for all residents of our global village.

Write for five minutes in your WJ on what you think our global society will look like in 2100.

Graceful-Aging Wisdom

To know how to grow old is the master work of wisdom, and one of the most difficult chapters in the great art of living.
— Henri-Frederic Amiel (1821–1881)

Growing old is not optional. Whether or not we grow old gracefully is. Science may help us retain our health; grace, however, is required for us to know how best to use the life and health that we have.

As in most things, our attitude is key. We all know people who are grown up in body but immature in their judgments and actions. Getting older by itself does not mean getting wiser, nor does wisdom come easily to most of us.

I am lucky. Because I skipped eighth grade, I was two, even three years younger than everybody else in boarding school. Now in my late 70s, my hair has turned white so the checkout clerks at supermarkets routinely ask if I need help out to the car. But all is not lost, I am also offered senior discounts on many things.

In his essay on aging, Cicero, senator and moralist during Rome's Golden Age, wrote, "For as I like a young man in whom there is something of the old, so I like an old man in whom there is something of the young; and he who follows this maxim, in body will possibly be an old man, but he will never be an old man in his mind." As Cicero suggests, growing old gracefully means staying young inside.

How are you coping with the prospect of getting older? In your WJ write on how you felt about your last big birthday.

Grateful Wisdom

If the only prayer you say in your entire life is "Thank you," that would suffice.
– Meister Eckhart (1260?–1327), Translated by Matthew Fox

Requests are hot, while thanks are cold. I'd spend hours crafting funding proposals, yet if a check came in, it took only five minutes for a pro-forma thank-you. My relationship with God is similar. I mainly send the Almighty lots of requests. Fortunately, now I also send thank-yous.

I was once praying with a friend from Seattle who owned a computer business and was looking for a knowledgeable associate. At a conference we were both at, he had asked if I would help him find the right person through prayer.

The way I approach directive prayer is pretty straightforward. I said something like, "God, if it's your will, please help so-and-so receive the assistance needed now for his business." I then asked to receive guidance in an image, word, or phrase accompanied by a feeling. In this case I kept repeating "thank you" and told my friend that based on what I had gotten, his problem had already been solved. In the meantime, he should just say, "Thank you."

That evening he told me that at lunch he had met a young man from Ohio with a master's degree in computer science, relevant experience, and plans to move to Seattle. Before the conference concluded, a deal had been struck, and the results are still positive. Thank you.

How do you express gratitude? For the coming week, every time you are about to ask for something, send the Universe a thank-you instead. Describe the process and results in your WJ.

Great-Life Wisdom

The only way to make contact with the Great Life, or the Power of God, is for a person really to surrender and let go. And this surrender must not be in word only, but must penetrate throughout their inner feeling until they truly feel they believe in, praise and worship no one but the One Almighty God.
— Muhammad Subuh Sumohadiwidjojo (1901–1987), *Susila Budhi Dharma*, 2001

I first encountered the Subud spiritual practice in Chicago in April, 1961. A newly minted Yale B.A. in English, I spent the year living with my parents while trying to figure out my next steps. A taxi driver named Raymond changed my life.

Subud, I learned from him, is an acronym based on three Sanskrit words: *Susila, budhi,* and *dharma.* Although the terms are from India, the spiritual practice they represent originated in Indonesia in 1924. The founder, Muhammad Subuh Sumohadiwidjojo (d. 1987), whom his followers call "Bapak" (father), described Subud as a way to live a noble life (*susila*) through surrendering (*dharma*) to one's highest self (*budhi*), our inner ambassador of the Great Life.

The practice consists of standing in a room alone or with others (men and women separated), then "receiving" for thirty minutes twice a week. Individuals are fully conscious as they sing, move, verbalize, or see internal images. This "exercise" resembles yawning in that whatever comes is spontaneous and unexpected. The results since May 1961 for this secular intellectual are deepened religious faith, strengthened intuition, and the awareness of God's continuing helpful presence in my everyday life.

Write in your WJ about how you are able to contact your deepest, best self.

Guru Wisdom

Gladly would he learn and gladly teach.
– Geoffrey Chaucer (1343–1400), describing one of the pilgrims
in *The Canterbury Tales*

In the Literature of Wisdom course I created in 1990, teaching and learning activities seemed to emerge naturally. Once I asked my adult students to point to the teacher. Most pointed to me. I then asked them to try again and be creative. This time more pointed to each other, about half pointed to themselves, a few pointed up or down, and I (joining in) pointed all around.

The "point" is that the more effective we are as learners, the more "teachers" we will find. Everyone and everything can educate. As the educator Harold Taylor wrote, the whole world can be our teacher.

The Hindu saying is pertinent: When the disciple is ready, the guru will appear. Now *guru* is no more—but also no less—than the Sanskrit word for *teacher*, and in India there are many kinds of gurus. At a gathering at the University of Hawaii in 1971, I remember the Indian sitar virtuoso Ravi Shankar talking about his guru. Shankar was referring to his music teacher.

One of the Javanese names for God is *Mahaguru*, the Great Teacher. If God is everywhere, then that which can teach us must be everywhere too: family, friends, lovers, pets, nature, even strangers we meet on airplanes. The kingdom of learning is within and all around. Finally, our greatest teacher may be ourselves. If we look inside, we'll usually find the answers we seek.

Write in your WJ about a learning experience which came from someone or something other than an official teacher.

Healing Wisdom

Jung spoke of the archetype called the wounded healer. I believe that each wound we suffer and eventually heal from is a soul-making experience with the potential to awaken our willingness to participate in the healing of the world.
— Joan Borysenko, Ph.D., *Fire in the Soul*, 1993

Heal... hale... whole... holy. To heal is to help another sentient being become healthy. "Hale and hardy" is the old-fashioned doublet for this state. Wholeness is a metaphor for good health, whether physical or mental. For Carl Jung, the goal of healing was psychic reintegration, restoring a broken person to wholeness. When we are unbroken, all-of-a-piece, we become like God: One. And that wholeness is holy.

The world, which we sometimes refer to as the "whole world," is one in body as are we. It is also divided by its human inhabitants into ethnic groups and nation-states that, unfortunately, have a history of not getting along. The Jewish tradition of *tikkun olam*, healing the world, is thus incumbent on us all. For the Earth is both Mother and Home. We need to respect it and make sure our descendants have a place to live in that's at least as good as ours.

Dr. Borysenko's point is that as we recover, we can become a source of recovery for others. Twelve Step sponsors are good examples. Having persevered in the Program, they can serve as role models and advisors for newer members. From the sick and wounded, it seems, God can make healers.

In your WJ list three things you can do to help heal the world.

Healthy-Eating Wisdom

We are what we eat.

– A common saying

When it comes to eating, the basic wisdom is, you eat to live. The next consideration has to do with quantity. The keynote is although we eat to live, we shouldn't live to eat. We need to limit what we consume to a reasonable amount. Too much of a good thing is no longer good. Whatever the body can't use and is unable to eliminate gets stored as fat. And the more fat we carry around, the worse for our health.

Wisdom has to do with the quality of our food as well. Here there is a whole variety of issues, some controversial. The American Heart Association and common sense recommend a balanced diet, with foods from all the major food groups. The food-pyramid model suggests how many servings from each group an individual should consume per day. These recommendations are updated periodically, even as health fads come and go.

Quality also concerns the healthiness of what we eat. Here things get murky: organic versus inorganic, combining certain foods with others, avoiding specific components (fats, sugars, caffeine, etc.), vegetarianism versus meat eating, veganism, eating gluten-free, selecting non-GMO foods, and so on. Concerns also surround when we eat, how much we chew, and our emotional state while eating.

Because people are different, we need to track, then follow, what works for us. In any case, eating wisely clearly requires serious consideration, increasing our food knowledge, discipline, persistence, and attention to labels. When healthy eating turns into fanaticism, however, we need to reconsider our priorities.

Discuss in your WJ your thoughts around food and healthy eating.

Heroic Wisdom

The hero-deed to be wrought is not today what it was in the century of Galileo. Where then there was darkness, now there is light; but also, where light was, there now is darkness. The modern hero-deed must be that of questing to bring to light again the lost Atlantis of the co-ordinated soul.

– Joseph Campbell (1904–1987), *The Hero with a Thousand Faces*, 1968

The late Joseph Campbell was a phrase-maker. *The Hero with a Thousand Faces*, the title of his most popular work, is an example. So is "the lost Atlantis of the co-ordinated soul."

The myth of Atlantis is premised on the ancient idea of a Golden Age succeeded by declining levels of social harmony and achievement until humankind destroyed itself. Then a small remnant began the long climb to a new Golden Age.

People who believe in Atlantis, Lemuria, and other ancient utopias hold that technology and spiritual development had reached the apex of development in tandem. Interstellar travel coexisted with ESP and the ability to converse with the gods. Then things somehow got out of whack. Spiritual maturity couldn't keep pace with technological progress, an imbalance which destroyed civilization, the utopias sinking to the bottom of the sea.

The "co-ordinated soul" is based on balance. When body, emotions, intellect, and spirit are rightly ordered, one's highest powers are in control. Campbell decried the modern imbalance favoring individuals over society—the head over the heart and soul. We too are flirting with self-destruction. The role of today's hero is thus helping rebalance our planet before we too self-destruct.

In your WJ describe someone you think exemplifies heroic wisdom today.

Historical Wisdom

Bill Moyers: Do you see any evidence that we really take away lessons... from the past... that cause us to change course before we hit the iceberg?
Vartan Gregorian [an Iranian-born Armenian-American academic serving in 2017 at 83 as president of Carnegie Corporation of New York]*: I absolutely do. But whether we're willing to change course or not—that's different.*
– Bill Moyers, A World of Ideas, 1989

"Those who cannot remember the past are condemned to repeat it," philosopher George Santayana (1863–1952) famously said. We attempt, individually, to learn from the past by getting to know elders and reading books. James Boswell (1740–1795), the most famous literary journal-keeper in English, used his, he said, to adjust his character. And Dr. Samuel Johnson, the subject of Boswell's famous biography, told Boswell that by studying others' lives, we could draw useful lessons and apply them to our own.

Historians provide us with the same kind of perspective on a larger scale. Another eighteenth-century Englishman, Edward Gibbon, attempted in his three-volume treatment to tease out the moral causes of the fall of Rome. A twentieth-century compatriot, Arnold Toynbee, studied the life cycles of civilizations.

Have we individually or collectively learned from the past? Or are we like Napoleon III, about whom historian A.J.P. Taylor commented, "Like most of those who study history, he learned from the mistakes of the past how to make new ones." The jury is still out. But I hope we never stop trying.

What major lesson do you think people in the twenty-first century will draw from the twentieth? Share your thoughts with your WJ.

Hospice Wisdom

Home is the one place where your own priorities hold sway.
— Dr. Atul Gawande, *Being Mortal*, 2014

When my first wife was told in June 2006 that she had stage 4B pancreatic cancer and only a few months to live, she was clear as the Honolulu afternoon through which we drove back from Kaiser Hospital. "I want to die at home with you, my books, and my cat close by," she said. And "I want the girls [our adult children] to come soon so that they can remember me looking fairly healthy."

The option was clear: we would do home hospice. We had a friend who had just become a social worker for the Saint Francis Hospice. When their intake nurse visited us, it turned out I knew her father. Medicare covered everything except $25 for an over-the-bed movable table. The nurse who came weekly had been doing this work in our valley for over 20 years, and it showed. Simone, who had become Catholic several weeks after her diagnosis, received Holy Communion daily. Our hospice volunteers were mainly all friends, including my Lions sister, the wife of the former Honolulu mayor, and a mother/daughter team, the latter of whom, a massage therapist, gave us both weekly massages.

Both daughters, our son-in-law, and six-year-old granddaughter arrived soon after diagnosis. The local CBS news anchor, a friend, did a 40-minute video of Simone, the kids, and me. Hospice totally controlled pain. Witnessing Simone's death felt like being at a birth. Hospice truly let her die peacefully at home.

What do you know about hospice? Write in your WJ on your views about this program.

Hospitable Wisdom

Sometimes give your services for nothing, calling to mind a previous benefaction or present satisfaction. And if there be an opportunity of serving one who is a stranger in financial straits, give full assistance to all such.

– Hippocrates (c. 460–377 BCE), Precepts

Generosity, hospitality, and charity are among the most commendable of human traits. Sometimes it is best just to give things away. Often at garage sales you will find boxes marked "free."

Nearly five centuries before Christ, Hippocrates advised physicians to serve those who could not pay, even strangers. The reason: The physicians themselves may have been in need, and a generous person may have helped them. In gratitude, generosity and hospitality are prescribed.

When I was a 19-year-old exchange student in Germany, people were often kind to me. A taxi driver in Heidelberg refused my fare because I had taken the trouble to learn his language. Frau Laupp, my landlady, did a superb job of washing and ironing my laundry, well beyond what was required by what I paid her. My friend Hans' parents took me in and treated me as part of the family during several vacations.

My wife and I welcome young people and others into our home to pass on the hospitality we ourselves have received. By returning the kindnesses we have experienced, we participate in a process of giving and receiving not unlike the rain cycle whereby water from the earth is stored in clouds, then returned to the land as life-giving rain.

Note in your WJ examples of hospitality you have given and received. How do you feel when you participate in them?

Immoderate Wisdom

Excess on occasion is exhilarating. It prevents moderation from acquiring the deadening effect of a habit.
                                  – W. Somerset Maugham (1874–1965)

The Ancient Greeks advocated the Golden Mean. Buddhism prizes the Middle Way. And Somerset Maugham makes the point that excessive moderation is also excessive. You *can* have too much of a good thing.

I prefer the Chinese concept of Yin and Yang. True moderation is the result of the interaction of extremes, not their avoidance. Our puritanical culture assumes that by staying away from the manic, we will keep ourselves safe from the depressive. This prescription is as foolish as not having fun in order to avoid being sad. Excessive moderation not only dulls, it deadens.

A good extreme once in a while is healthy for body and soul. Think of staying up really late on New Year's Eve, going out on a special occasion to an excellent but very expensive restaurant, dancing until dawn, or treating yourself one day to that dream vacation. On six days thou shalt watch thy step and live moderately, but on the seventh thou shalt let out all the stops, take risks, and let nothing prevent you from having fun.

Some of us know this truth with regard to our own lives. In consequence we try to balance hard work with hard play, activity with leisure. But in case we don't, we should remember that when it comes to living moderately, we should do so with moderation.

Can you kick up your heels every now and then and really go all out? Discuss in your WJ how good you are at living life to the fullest.

Impeccable Wisdom

You should learn to live the impeccable life of a warrior.
– Don Juan's advice to Carlos in Castaneda's Journey
To Ixtlan, 1972

When World War II ended, my future wife of 43 years, Simone (1931–2006), was just fourteen. With her mother and older sister, she had fled from the oncoming Russian front in East Prussia, then the remotest part of Germany. When the family finally arrived in Munich, they had only the clothes on their backs, some baby things, a few photo albums, and an address. They were lucky to be alive.

I think Carlos Castaneda's mentor, the Yaqui Indian sorcerer Don Juan Matus, would have found Simone an "impeccable warrior." In 1950 she attended secretarial school by day and worked at the village movie theater by night. The job didn't pay much, but work was scarce. One evening her new leather wallet was stolen from the projection booth. The wallet, a gift, had contained forty marks, a lot of money then, plus irreplaceable family photos. She cried and prayed.

Two weeks later the wallet was recovered. Only the money was missing. One night while cleaning the theater, she found another wallet, this one bulging with bills plus an ID card. The owner was contacted. The next evening a well-dressed man approached her. "Excuse me, Fräulein. Thank you for finding my wallet. I understand that yours was recently taken and you lost forty marks. I'd like to give you these forty marks for finding mine." Don Juan might have commented that the universe had approved of Simone's impeccability.

In your WJ describe an occasion when you acted "impeccably." What was the outcome?

Inclusive Wisdom

Some Christians speak not only of the "uniqueness" of Christ but of the "exclusiveness." ... It cannot be said too plainly, however, that exclusivity is utterly contrary to the Jesus we meet in the synoptic Gospels... Jesus did not see "Christianity" and "Judaism." ... He saw faith.

– Diana L. Eck, *Encountering God*, 1993

Encountering God is one of the best books on religion I've ever read. Dr. Diana Eck, professor of Comparative Religion and Indian Studies at Harvard, writes about her initial encounter with Hinduism. A Methodist from Bozeman, Montana, she had never met a non-Christian until her freshman year at Smith. When she went to Varanasi (Benares), India, in 1965, she experienced the first challenge to her beliefs. It came not through books or ideas but from "Hindus whose lives were a powerful witness to their faith."

The major Abrahamic religions all tend to exclusiveness. You are either a Jew, Christian, or Muslim. Christianity and Islam are religions that claim to have the Truth, and both go about seeking converts. Hindus, Buddhists, and Taoists, on the other hand, are unlikely to press others to convert or to condemn them for not joining their religion.

I agree with Professor Eck that a God of love, as manifested in Jesus' life and sacrifice, cannot be exclusive. When Jesus asked God from the cross to pardon the Jewish religious officials who had condemned him, he might also have been speaking for us latter-day followers of God's truth. "Forgive us, God. Sometimes we really don't know what we're doing."

Write in your WJ how you regard people of other faiths.

Inner-Hearing Wisdom

Wonders are many, and none is more wonderful than man.
                                    – Sophocles (c. 496–406 BCE), *Antigone*

In 1824 Beethoven's *Ninth Symphony* was first performed in Vienna. Known as "The Choral," the *Ninth* sets to music Friedrich Schiller's "Ode to Joy," familiar to churchgoers as the basis for the uplifting English hymn *Joyful, Joyful, We Adore Thee.* What makes Beethoven's accomplishment amazing is that the composer was completely deaf when he wrote the *Ninth Symphony.*

You might well ask, how in the world a deaf person could compose melodies pleasing and impressive to those who can hear? Or how could Helen Keller, who was blind as well as deaf, learn to read, then write in rich, graceful prose? How indeed!

Given the myriad stimuli of our outer environment, we can easily forget something important—that there is also a rich inner world. We *can* see with our eyes closed, as anyone who dreams knows. So, it makes sense that the same sort of thing can happen to those who cannot hear.

Beethoven was not born deaf. Perhaps he simply remembered what a beautiful melody looked like on paper. Perhaps the visual architecture of the music translated into something equally pleasing to his inner ear. The concept is fascinating—the possibility that we have inner as well as outer hearing. That we can "hear" even if we are deaf, "see" even if we are blind. Whatever the case, the extent of our human capacities truly inspires wonder. Sophocles is right: Of the many wonders on earth, none is more wonderful than humankind.

Have you ever heard an inner voice? Describe the experience in your WJ.

Inner-Knowing Wisdom

If you do not find the Wisdom and Mystery of life within yourself, you surely will never find it without.
– From the "Charge of the Goddess," quoted in *Virgin, Mother, Crone* by Donna Wilshire, 1995

In 19th-century novels, the way to recover from a deep disappointment was to travel abroad. This idea was expressed in the phrase "to get away from it all."

When I was 18, I left the United States for the first time on my own as a Yale-Heidelberg exchange student. Although I had lived away from home before, this trip would be different. Spending a year on my own as an American Jew in Germany 13 years after World War II was not the same as going to an American boarding school or college. Those 12 months comprised the richest year of my life. I learned among other things that in both Germany and America there were people I liked, people I didn't, and many toward whom I had no particular feeling. Intellectually I already knew that people are people wherever they are, but now I knew this reality from experience.

Today I believe we all have wisdom. Our souls already know that people everywhere are people regardless of outer differences. Children are in touch with this inner knowing and have no trouble playing with peers from another race or culture. Soon they are socialized to play only with their own kind. If they are lucky, however, their inner knowing one day reasserts itself, and they throw off the shackles of such small-minded notions.

Write in your WJ how your inner wisdom helped you overcome some limiting belief.

Inspirational Wisdom

The music of this opera [Madame Butterfly] was dictated to me by God; I was merely instrumental in putting it on paper and communicating it to the public.

– Giacomo Puccini (1858–1924)

What is the source of inspiration? Where do ideas—artistic, musical, literary, or scientific—come from? An experience of my daughter Marianna, who has a degree in art as well as two in English literature, may prove helpful. We were looking for a logo for "Blue Sky Associates: Catalysts for Educational Change," the nonprofit consulting group several of us had started. Marianna sat quietly for a few minutes, then sketched part of the arc of the sun with blue rays of different lengths emanating from it. The idea was simple and brilliant. When I asked how she came up with this concept, she answered, "It was what I saw after I got quiet."

Purposive thinking can lead to writer's cramp or a headache. By contrast, meditating, doing sports, dancing, or watching an enjoyable movie can clear the mind and make a space for spirit to work. That is what *in-spiration* means: the in-flowing or in-dwelling of spirit. When we are too full of our ordinary ego self, we have no room for our deepest God-connected self to function. Artists of all kinds learn to get out of the way so that their creativity can enter and work.

Scientists find answers this way too. After dozens of failures, Edison discovered in a dream how to make a successful incandescent lightbulb. Dreams are another state where our ordinary thinking selves are suspended.

In your WJ write about the role inspiration plays in your life.

Interfaith Wisdom

I appreciate any organization or individual people who sincerely make an effort to promote harmony between humanity, and particularly harmony between the various religions. I consider it very sacred work and very important work.

– His Holiness the 14th Dalai Lama

My religious background is unusual. I grew up in a secular middle-class Jewish family. My parents and sister never went to temple. I, however, had Florene, our long-time black housekeeper, a Methodist, who hummed hymns in the kitchen and told me about Jesus. At 11, I began attending an American [Northern] Baptist boarding school. As an undergraduate, I attended by turns an Episcopal church, Yale's Congregational chapel, and on occasion the Hillel Shabbat services. Baptized with my infant daughter, now 51, I spent 37 years as a (liberal) Lutheran, my first wife's faith; seven as a Roman Catholic; and the last six as an Episcopalian. Meantime, I have been a devoted follower of the contemplative Subud practice for nearly 57 years while also studying Shamanism, Confucianism, Taoism, Hinduism, and Buddhism on the side.

As non-religious individuals often point out, so much evil has been done in the name of religions. One only need think of the Crusades of the Middle Ages or of militant Jihads today. In World War I both the Axis forces and the Allies carried banners declaring "God with Us." Even Buddhists, generally considered peaceful by comparison with followers of other faiths, have shown their all-too-human side in cruelly attacking the Rohingya minority in Myanmar.

Frankly, I hope my interfaith commitment foreshadows a future of religious universalism, not conflict.

In your WJ discuss your views on multi-faith religiosity.

Interracial-Marriage Wisdom

All differences in this world are of degree, and not of kind, because oneness is the secret of everything.
                  – Swami Vivekananda (1863–1902)

A May 2017 report from the Pew Research Center indicated that Honolulu, Hawaii, at 42%, had the highest interracial marriage rate of any city in the United States. The Aloha State clearly walks its talk. Second came the Las Vegas-Henderson-Paradise region of Nevada, at 31%. The national average, at 17%, was already significantly higher than its 3% rate when the U.S. Supreme Court ruled against marital segregation by race in 1967. We've clearly come quite a way.

How long, though, will it take the people of the world to realize that we human beings all belong to the same race, the human one? If that were not so, we would not be able to have children across the so-called racial divides. What cat mother would forbid her white cat-daughter from mating with a black tom, or vice versa? We call ourselves the highest animal, but you really have to wonder sometimes.

I am not arguing here against individuals marrying or partnering with others from their same racial, ethnic, or religious groups. When I was an exchange student in Heidelberg, Germany, in 1958-59, however, I had the good fortune to hear the great historian Arnold Toynbee deliver a lecture in British-accented German. World peace would only come, he thought, when one of two conditions obtained: We had a smoothly functioning, efficient world government, or there was mass intermarriage across every conceivable boundary. The latter, he thought, was more likely.

What's your view of interracial marriage? Write about it in your WJ.

IQ-Versus-EQ Wisdom

If your emotional abilities aren't in hand... then no matter how smart you are, you are not going to get very far.
— Dr. Daniel Goleman

In 1995 psychologist Goleman caused a stir with his book *Emotional Intelligence*. His basic point was that cognitive intelligence isn't enough. Goleman stated that emotional intelligence, or EQ, often matters more than IQ. Because most of us have sometimes been pretty dumb smart people, his conclusion should come as no surprise.

I once wrote an article entitled "The Educated Person—What Does That Mean?" I argued that education should take account of humanity's complex learning needs. I postulated that "the holistically educated person will not be measured by IQ alone but by BQ (Body Quotient), EQ (Emotion Quotient), and SQ (Spirit Quotient) as well."

The idea of a diversely developed human being is not new. Horace talked about a sound mind in a sound body. In the late nineteenth century, Rudolf Steiner emphasized educating the imagination, voice, and body as much as the intellect.

In the 1920s G.I. Gurdjieff established a school in France for the "harmonious development of man [sic]," integrating body, emotions, and intellect to produce a fully mature human being.

Clearly, to reach our full potential, we need to go beyond our IQ. Why be an intellectual giant and an emotional dwarf? I would add another Q—our Wisdom Quotient. For if all our other indicators are high but our WQ remains low, how can we improve ourselves or our society?

In your WJ brainstorm criteria against which to measure your various Qs. Which Q is the most important to you?

Know-Nothing Wisdom

The only thing that we can know is that we know nothing and that is the highest flight of human wisdom.

– Leo Tolstoy (1828–1910)

One problem with citing something another person has written is that you may not know the original context. Is the above a thought Tolstoy himself entertained, or is it the opinion of one of his fictional characters? For our purposes, the sentiment is what matters, and a pessimistic sentiment it is: We human beings apparently can know nothing, and arriving at this "fact" is the ultimate reach of our wisdom. A similar conclusion drove Goethe's Faust to give himself to the Devil.

Human wisdom seems to come in two kinds: the worldly variety and the spiritual type. Benjamin Franklin is a well-known dispenser of the former; the Buddha is a fountainhead of the latter. Both kinds have their usefulness. To the extent that all of us must live in this world, it helps to know that a penny saved is a penny earned. But when it comes to transcendent questions of life and death, worldly wisdom remains earthbound and insufficient.

Our efforts to resolve deep mysteries of the latter type on our own will lead us to a conclusion similar to that of Tolstoy. Wisdom of the transcendent kind belongs to God. Fortunately, God seems willing to share divine wisdom with the least of us to the extent that we are able to humble ourselves and hear it. Admitting our ignorance may thus be the first and most important step to gaining wisdom.

Have you ever felt that you know nothing? Write about the experience in your WJ.

Laughing Wisdom

A day without laughter is a day wasted.
– Charlie Chaplin (1889–1977)

When a priest in our church called to ask if we knew of someone who could take in an African gentleman seeking political asylum in the United States, we had no idea how much we would learn from this individual or how good a friend he would become. First, however, he became our house guest.

The individual in question, a gentle giant of a man, just 44, had been a high official in his war-torn country. Prior to that he had studied for the Catholic priesthood in Rome and had managed along the way to acquire two master's degrees, both from England. Instead of the ministry, he entered the military and rose to the rank of major general. When he started serving as the rallying point for the opposition to the corrupt government in his country, however, he became a *persona non grata* and had to leave home quickly. His wife and four small children, meanwhile, went into hiding. Fortunately, he now knows where they are and that they are safe. For a long time, though, he didn't.

What an example he is for laughing in the face of adversity. For example, he is still waiting after many months to learn whether he has received political asylum. Yet he laughs almost all the time, keeps things light, and helps the rest of us, with many fewer difficulties and cares on our plates, to do the same. We members of the Boulder community are blessed to know him, and now you are too.

Write in your WJ about your capacity for laughter.

Leaving-Home Wisdom

One doesn't discover new lands without consenting to lose sight of the shore for a very long time.

— Andre Gide (1869–1951)

Leaving home is a Biblical imperative (Gen. 2:24). Now you might reply that the Bible talks about "a man" having to leave father and mother; nothing is said about a woman. But it seems easier for female adult children to return to their parents than for their male siblings. Young men, once out on their own, seem to think their tires will be wrecked if they reverse direction.

Moreover, men alas still earn more than women, and mothers are usually left with the children when a relationship breaks up. No wonder women go home — it's the place, as poet Robert Frost once wrote — where they have to take you in.

Home has all the plusses and minuses of the womb. It's nice and cozy but also restrictive. You don't have to do anything, but then you can't do anything. You don't have to pay, but you don't have a say. Sooner or later you leave. Ultimately there's no free lunch.

The greatest limitation of home is that it offers only one officially sanctioned way of being in the world. That may be the best for most of us, but we'll never know until we get out on our own and compare it with other modes of living.

So, we are left with casting off for a far country and perhaps never coming home. Yet herein lies a paradox. For, like the prodigal son, in losing ourselves we may just find ourselves.

Write about your experience of leaving home in your WJ.

Legislative Wisdom

O God, the fountain of wisdom, whose statutes are good and gracious... guide and bless the Legislature of this State, that it may ordain for our governance only such things as [serve] the welfare of the people... Amen.

– From "A Prayer for a State Legislature," *Book of Common Prayer*, 1789

The Elizabethan cadences of Thomas Cranmer (1489–1556), the initial Protestant Archbishop of Canterbury, survived the American Revolution and are found in America's first Episcopal prayer book. Although the terminology and content differ from the original version published by Cranmer in 1549, later editions have retained the elegant word flow that makes this book a pinnacle of English prose.

American, of course, is the reference to state legislatures. True democratic deliberative bodies did not exist in Cranmer's day. This prayer highlights one aspect of the separation between church and state in America, where a particular religion is not to be established. While the state is to remain secular, different faiths are free to invoke the deity to aid and guide government. Lord knows, the people's representatives, then and now, need as much help as they can get.

For religious people, God is the source of all wisdom, and God's statutes, based on truth, are universally beneficial. The same does not generally hold for human regulations. Taking the long view or considering the big picture are characteristics of the best public servants in a secular republic. Given our all-too-human nature, however, prayer for wise governance remains a good idea.

What is your view of "legislative wisdom"? In your WJ briefly discuss what you think sage governance would entail.

Liberation Wisdom

When I walked out of prison, that was my mission, to liberate the oppressed and the oppressor both. Some say that has now been achieved... [It is] but the first step on a longer and even more difficult road. For to be free is not merely to cast off one's chains, but to live in a way that respects and enhances the freedom of others.
– Nelson Mandela (1918–2013), *Long Walk to Freedom*, 1994

Back in the 1960s, Erich Fromm helped us distinguish between "freedom to" and "freedom from." "Freedom from" means we have escaped from a situation that has imprisoned or limited us. "Freedom to" means we are now in the position—psychologically, socially, politically, or economically—to do things differently, to become "a new person."

The issue of substance abuse illustrates the point. That a person has stopped drinking isn't the same thing as being sober. That's why the cessation of drinking is only the condition for admission to Alcoholics Anonymous. The program itself focuses on personal transformation. Freedom from drinking is merely a prologue to becoming someone who no longer needs to drink. The Twelve Steps and other tools of the program are the means by which recovering alcoholics achieve that goal.

Nelson Mandela, one of the great leaders of the twentieth century, knew this distinction. Further, he understood that both oppressed and oppressor must be transformed, because the same system imprisons both. Fortunately, his spirit could never be shackled despite the years he spent as a prisoner on Robben Island. His wisdom can help liberate us all.

In your WJ discuss your idea of true freedom.

Lifelong-Learning Wisdom

Wisdom is not a product of schooling but of the lifelong attempt to acquire it.

– Albert Einstein (1879–1955)

Even though I once taught a course called "The Literature of Wisdom," it might be said that wisdom is unteachable, even unlearnable. At best, wisdom may be caught, not taught.

Look at the hard time Jesus had with what my former pastor liked to call the "duh-sciples." There they were, front-row witnesses to his miracles. They were even empowered to do some of their own during his lifetime. Yet they never seemed fully to believe in him or comprehend who he was.

For anyone who has had a hard time in school, it is heartening to learn that geniuses like Einstein and Edison either dropped out or were kicked out of school. In traditional schools, teachers represent the authority of the older generation. They seem to know what's what, and it's the student's job not to question but to accept whatever they offer up as truth. Students are not encouraged to present divergent ideas or tap their native wisdom.

Fortunately, each of us also attends the larger school of life. It continues as long as we do, tuition is free, and special admission programs are unnecessary. We all get individualized tutoring, and every class has a required lab. According to one theory, we have to retake courses until we master the material. It is a cause for hope that no less a personage than Albert Einstein thought attendance in this school might eventually help us become wise.

In your WJ discuss how the School of Life has given you a measure of wisdom.

Lost-and-Found Wisdom

For this people's heart has become calloused;
they hardly hear with their ears and they have closed
their eyes. Otherwise they might see with their eyes,
hear with their ears, [and] understand with their
hearts.

– Matthew 13:15–17 (NIV)

Wisdom is everywhere, but we have to be able to find it.

My wife is a finder. By contrast after looking for something without success for a few minutes, I get tired or bored and give up. "Where's the X?" I'll yell. She'll then open the fridge; go right to the place I've just been looking at; and, lo and behold, there to my consternation she finds the missing item.

To commemorate my seeming inability to find even the most obvious things, she recently showed me a *New Yorker* cartoon of a husband looking at a fridge full of butter as he calls out to his wife, "Honey, where's the butter?"

Wisdom is like that—ubiquitous, universal, but often invisible. To the blind there are neither sunrises nor sunsets. We need the gift of sight, or in the case of wisdom, insight.

President Obama in the final summit of his presidency, with Japanese Prime Minister Abe at the Pearl Harbor Memorial in Honolulu in late-December 2016, said that the past cannot be changed. What we have to do is draw the pertinent lessons from it so as not to repeat the same mistakes.

May we each become finders like my wife—not just of butter or misplaced cellphones but of wisdom. For those with the eyes to see, it's everywhere.

Write in your WJ about what you learned from losing then finding something.

Mainland Wisdom

No man [sic] is an island, entire of itself; every man is a piece of the continent, a part of the main... Therefore never send to know for whom the bell tolls. It tolls for thee.

– John Donne (1572–1631)

Hawaii, a far-flung mini-archipelago stretching over a thousand miles, consists of very little land. It's geographically among the smallest of the fifty states. Even the "Big Island" is but a pebble in a vast sea. Many Hawaiian residents hail from a mainland— North American or Asian. When capitalized, the term refers to the continental United States. A New Yorker, I lived happily in Honolulu for 17 years.

The John Donne excerpt, above, ranks with the 23rd Psalm, the Sermon on the Mount, and Hamlet's "'To be, or not to be" soliloquy as one of the most famous passages in English. At least two subsequent book titles derive from it. Yet the sentiment expressed is even more important.

As human beings we seem separate individuals, islands of our personal needs, locked up in our heads. But the act of procreation shows that this is not our true situation. Even artificial insemination requires a sperm donor, a host, and a team of medical specialists. Every person and company are dependent on a large network of others just to function. Really *knowing* that each of us is a part of the whole, members of the human family, coparticipants in the ecosystem, interdependent neighbors of the plants and animals makes us citizens of the world. John Donne really said it all.

Do you consider yourself a world citizen? Why? Why not? Respond in your WJ.

Majority Wisdom

A man with God is always in the majority.
— John Knox (1505–1572)

The world is coming, slowly but surely, to majority rule. That said, we can't forget that China, the most populous nation on the planet, remains a "People's Republic" in name only. Still, more and more countries have adopted democratic systems in recent years. Near-universal access to basic education, television, computers, and social media is developing a literate electorate with some sense of global issues.

Not that the majority is always right. Critics of democracy from Plato to the present point out that the masses can generally be manipulated by demagogues. Still, in democracies contending parties can each use techniques of persuasion to sway voters, whereas in authoritarian states, only the group in power can do so. To paraphrase Winston Churchill, democracy is the worst form of government except for all the others.

There are also problems with the majority-of-one idea. Anybody can allege a special mission from God. Dictators seem especially prone to asserting their unique place in history, whether from God or Destiny. Jesus specifically warned us to watch out for false messiahs. Fortunately, good leaders need not advertise their virtues. Those alive in the early 21st century were fortunate to have breathed the same air for a while with the likes of Nelson Mandela, Archbishop Tutu, Mother Teresa, Pope Francis, and the Dalai Lama. These outstanding human beings and leaders don't have to toot their own horns. Their stature and wisdom are evident to the majority of us.

What is your viewpoint on majority rule in the Age of Donald Trump? Discuss this matter in your WJ.

Manna-from-Heaven Wisdom

The LORD said to Moses, "I will rain down bread from heaven for you. Each day the people shall go out and gather a day's supply, so that I can put them to the test and see whether they will follow my instructions or not."

– Exodus 16:4–5

A main Biblical theme is that God will take care of us. A related theme is we will be tested. I have experienced both.

After getting fired from a university vice presidency in 1990, I had little more than a year to find another job. Since I had excellent credentials and good experience, I felt certain I would find one. But there's not much room at the top. In a search attracting 150 candidates, I generally made the semifinals or was a finalist. In the case of a small-college presidency, it came down to one other person and me. When I received the bad news, the caller said, "You should be proud. There were 250 candidates, and you came in second." No joy there—I had followed all the instructions but no manna rained down.

After a year with no job, I became a consultant, taught courses, wrote a book, and took out and repaid loans as necessary. Somehow we survived. At Christmas we still had our house, and in time things got better. It wasn't a steak dinner, but the manna did fall.

I still worry sometimes, but I am better about it now. Experience is a stern master but a good teacher.

Have you received manna from heaven? Write in your WJ what you have learned from your hard times.

Meaningful Wisdom

An old day passes, a new day arrives. The important thing is to make it... a meaningful day.

– H. H. the Dalai Lama

My church, St. John's Episcopal in Boulder, has established what's called an Intentional Community. Eight of us meet Sunday afternoons from 3:00 to 4:30pm. We begin by adjourning from our library/conference room to the nearby Holy Family Chapel. There, after someone has given an opening reading, often a brief Bible passage, we do 15 minutes of Centering Prayer. For those unfamiliar with the term, it's a form of meditation developed by Fr. Thomas Keating, a Cistercian monk and priest, which is widely practiced today in Catholic and mainstream Protestant communities. Next, one of us conducts an abridged evening service from the New Zealand Book of Common Prayer. When that's over, we return to our meeting room for the remaining hour to discuss a common reading or to listen and react to a member's spiritual update.

At our last meeting, Kathy S., an octogenarian still actively practicing psychotherapy, told us that from her decades of work with clients, she found the underlying cause of their discontent was a lack of meaningfulness in their lives.

She had an important insight. Socrates insisted that the unexamined life was not worth living. One might also posit that a life devoid of meaning is equally empty. These two ideas are linked. If we examine our lives periodically and find them lacking in meaning, we need to correct course. Hopefully this book can help with the navigation.

Are you able to find meaning in life's daily challenges? Respond in your WJ.

Midlife-Crisis Wisdom

Midway through this life of ours
I found myself in a dark wood
Where the right path was unclear.
        – Dante Alighieri (1265–1321), *The Divine Comedy*
                    (coauthor's translation)

We create age benchmarks for ourselves: 18, 21, 30, 35, the Big Four-O, then 65 or 70. Our fortieth birthday is especially significant because it signals the halfway point in our life expectancy. No longer young adults, we may have children of our own. For childless women, the biological clock ticks loudly. Or if we are still uncertain about our career, when will we finally figure out "what we were meant to do"? Time is starting to run out for everything.

I have a friend who threw an incredible fortieth birthday party for herself. A bright, attractive woman, she was friendly, articulate, a gifted salesperson. In her twenties she had made money by selling jewelry at swap-meets. But forty hit hard. She had everything—a good job, a nice apartment, a pleasant lifestyle, a loving family of origin. But she also had nothing: no life partner, kids, or assurance that she was really applying her talents. A few months later, within two days of each other, she was diagnosed with fibroid growths in her uterus and lost her job. Facing a midlife crisis, she prayed for guidance.

Dante's masterwork is entitled *The Divine Comedy* because, though it begins in darkness, it ends in light. Sometimes we have to lose our way to find it. For those with faith, a midlife crisis can also lead to a midcourse correction.

Write in your WJ about how a dark time in your life led you to greater enlightenment.

Mindful Wisdom

*The ultimate value of life depends upon awareness and the power of
contemplation rather than upon mere survival.*
— Aristotle (c. 384–322 BCE)

The journey from darkness to light, known as the process of
enlightenment, is often described as an awakening. The Sufis speak
about the three states of being asleep, aware, and awake. From a
spiritual perspective, most of us are fast asleep; some are aware of
a more conscious state toward which they are striving; and a very
small number are actually awake.

Taoist philosopher Chuang-tze once posed this question: "Am I
Chuang-tze dreaming he is a butterfly, or a butterfly dreaming he
is Chuang-tze?" The only way to find out, presumably, is to wake
up.

Knowing where we are, where we are going, and where the
obstacles lie is essential for reaching our human potential. We have
to be attentive and fully conscious to be able to discern what is
really important from that which only appears so. Adopting the
Zen technique of "single-pointedness" and mindfully focusing all
our attention on what we are doing at the moment will help.

Western values suggest that the more things we can do at a
time, the more accomplished we will be. Multitasking has become
the norm. Still, how much stress does it cause?

Perhaps it would be wise for us to begin our day with the Unity
Church's affirmation: "I am alive, alert, awake and enthusiastic
about my life"; then go forward with awareness to do what lies
before us.

*How awake or mindful are you? In your WJ reflect on a few ways you
might increase awareness in your daily life.*

Misfortunate Wisdom

Yield not to misfortunes but press forward the more boldly in their face.

— Virgil (70–19 BCE), *The Aeneid*, VI, 95

Commercial airline pilots have always impressed me with their ability to make those big, heavy machines take us to our destination even through air turbulence, clear-air or otherwise. It is obvious that pilots know the tolerance of their planes to handle the "bumps in the road," as a fearful-flier handbook I once read put it. Given the knowledge that pilots have, the best way around (with the exception of thunderstorms) is generally flying straight through. Sit back, relax, and don't worry about those periodic dips and yaws, they tell us in worry-free, laconic voices. In pilot talk, "It's just a little light chop."

I do distinguish between *misfortunes*, or episodes of turbulence in our lives, and *catastrophe*, which may be more accurately described as plane crashes or at least emergency landings. Life is filled with turbulence, from mild to severe. A long-time frequent flier, I am still around—a fact demonstrating turbulence to be a natural, fairly innocuous occurrence. Still, I have clear memories of extremely bumpy flights where everyone seemed to be praying and even a few screamed.

Wisdom indicates that we should face the obstacles in our lives and keep going. Virgil's Trojan hero, Aeneas, overcame his and, according to legend, founded Rome, with his father, Anchises, perched gingerly on his shoulders. Courage and perseverance will likely help us achieve our life's mission as well.

Give an example in your WJ of a time you faced and overcame misfortune, or when it defeated or derailed you. What lessons did you learn?

Monastic Wisdom

One of the first things I noticed on my longer retreats, when I was with the monks in choir four or five times a day for a week or more, was how like an exercise class the liturgy seemed... When I compared all this to an aerobics class, a monk said, "That's exactly right."

– Kathleen Norris, Dakota: A Spiritual Geography, 1993

I have been on a number of Catholic retreats, including a week at a Benedictine monastery, and have spent two weeks as the guest of a senior nun in a convent.

My Jewish Quaker friend Joe Engelberg went on regular retreats at the Trappist monastery in Gethsemane, Kentucky, Thomas Merton's monastic home. Joe was a quiet person, a happy combination of his basic personality plus years of Quaker formation. As for me, an addictive talker—a friend calls me *prolix*—being silent for twenty-four hours might produce a spiritual experience for someone else nearby!

Reading Father Merton's or Kathleen Norris' writings provides a taste of the work required and the aerobic-type "high" resulting from monastic observances. Yet *high* is probably the wrong word. It must be more like the contentment of a person able to let go and let God take the controls on a regular basis. In a talk I once attended, the speaker defined a saint as someone able to subordinate his or her will to God's on a daily basis. Monastic living strikes me as a support group for attaining this goal.

Have you ever attended a spiritual retreat or wanted to? In your WJ write about your experience or what you anticipate from it.

Money Wisdom

Having money in the bank gives one a sense of Buddhistic calm.

– Ayn Rand (1905–1982)

Money is usually overrated, yet we live in a money-oriented society. As the Beatles' song reminds us, it can't buy us love. And as the Bible tells us, "The love of money is the root of all evil... " (1 Timothy 6:10).

People like me tend to underrate money. As a student of the humanities, and a religious one to boot, I put money way down on my list of values. Moreover, I had an early prejudice against money. First, my father was a businessman. Dinner-table discussions often turned on how much—in dollar terms—someone was *worth*. By contrast, I tended to value people on how nice, interesting, or funny they were.

Second, our family was Jewish. Early on I learned that Jews were supposed to be interested only in money. Well, it did seem that way at our house. So, I took a private vow that money wasn't going to be my idol in life. Later, when my family made sure I got the best education money could buy, I felt pressure to go into business or another high-paying profession. How disappointed my parents were when their son the doctor chose to operate on nineteenth-century American fiction!

Now in my late-70s, I am content that I did not enter a career just to make money. On the other hand, I wish I had been a better steward of what I did make. A more balanced view of money would have served me and my family better.

In your WJ discuss your attitude toward money.

Moral-Leadership Wisdom

Mohandas Gandhi is my choice for Person of the Century because he... demonstrated that we can force change and justice through moral acts of aggression instead of physical acts of aggression. Never has our species needed this wisdom more.
– Steve Jobs (1955–2011), Cofounder of Apple Computer Inc.,
in *Time*, April 12, 1999

Gandhi was killed when I was eight, but I had a sense of him even as a child. He was a kind of Mother Teresa and Dalai Lama rolled into one. He was my first hero from the East.

I must have read his autobiography, *The Story of My Experiments with Truth* (1929), as a graduate student. Later I taught it in a Literature of Wisdom class. The West rediscovered Gandhi when Sir Richard Attenborough's Academy-Award-winning film came out in 1982.

In 1969 Arnold Toynbee, the distinguished British historian, honored the hundredth anniversary of Gandhi's birth by publishing an article on the significance of the latter's life and work. Toynbee asserted that Gandhi was a saint precisely because he wasn't afraid to tarnish his halo by working in the moral slums of politics. Gandhi's self-development, his strength of character and resolve, and his willingness to put his life on the line enabled him to know where and how to provide political and moral pressure for a positive outcome. All this made him uniquely effective in winning India's independence from Great Britain without extensive bloodshed.

The world's problems today beg for more Gandhian leaders to help solve them.

Obtain a copy of the movie Gandhi *and watch it. Comment in your WJ on its implications for your life.*

Neighborly Wisdom

He that lacks wisdom despises his neighbor, but a man of understanding holds his peace.

– Proverbs 11:12

Judeo-Christianity has a strong tradition of neighborliness. As far as Christianity goes, there are two major requirements: to love God and to love one's neighbors and treat them as we would be treated. The Golden Rule is all about relating with our neighbors.

When the lawyer asks Jesus to define who falls into that category, the latter tells the parable of the Good Samaritan (Luke 10:25–37). The phrase itself is an oxymoron. Although the Samaritans were ethnic Jews, their form of Judaism diverged in important respects from the mainstream variety in Jesus' day. According to catholic. com, "Because of their imperfect adherence to Judaism and their partly pagan ancestry, the Samaritans were despised by ordinary Jews." The concept of a *good* Samaritan would seem impossible to Jesus' contemporaries. Yet for Jesus the hated Samaritan in the story is more neighborly to the wounded Jew than either the priest or Levite.

When we judge our neighbors harshly, we typically see the speck in their eye while remaining unaware of the wood splinter in our own. If we are wise enough to know ourselves and human nature well, we will refrain from gossiping about or criticizing others. Instead, we'll use that same energy to improve who we are. Criticizing less and reflecting more will help us become good neighbors to both ourselves and others.

Monitor for one day the critical things you think and say about your neighbors and others. Reflect in your WJ on what you have observed and how you might change for the better.

Nominal Wisdom

Each child is named at birth, but it is understood that as a person develops, the birth name will be outgrown... Hopefully one's name will change several times in a lifetime as wisdom, creativity and purpose also become more clearly defined with time.
                    – Marlo Morgan, *Mutant Message Down Under*, 1991

My younger daughter was born Christine Jacqueline Feldman. In elementary school she was Tina and in middle school Chris for a while. In high school she announced she wanted to be called Christine. Meanwhile her stage name as a rock musician was Christine Darling. Now married and a Ph.D., she is Dr. Christine Feldman-Barrett.

Many cultures require different names for children and adults. Names sometimes signify new assignments. In the Bible, Abram becomes Abraham, Sarai Sarah, Simon Peter, etc. Members of religious orders often take new names. Orthodox Jews change the names of sickly children to fool the Angel of Death. Japanese, Chinese, Hungarians, and Bavarians give pride of place to the family by putting last names first.

My spiritual guide frequently gave followers new first names more in accord, he felt, with their inner natures. The names would be like personal mantras for them. Every time these names were repeated, he believed, would thus be like a prayer for the individuals to grow into their real, best selves. My birthnames were Stephen Michael, but I'm now Reynold Ruslan. While *Reynold* is my legal name, *Ruslan* incorporates both Christianity and Islam—a good thing in this religiously divided world.

In your WJ discuss how you feel about your name—its origin and any changes to it over time.

Non-Judgmental Wisdom

*Men [sic] of true wisdom and goodness are contented to take persons
and things as they are, without complaining of their imperfections,
or attempting to amend them.*
— Henry Fielding (1707–1754), *The History of Tom Jones: A
Foundling*, 1749

Fielding's "comic epic in prose" is filled with characters and
situations that teach us about wisdom and folly. Squire Allworthy is
the book's touchstone for virtue, generosity, and good sense. Since
encountering him in college, I have met some Squire Allworthys in
real life. For whatever reasons, all grew up in the United Methodist
Church. One I was fortunate to have had as my boss for a time.
Another was my senior-year prep-school roommate. A third
almost became governor of South Dakota. While not a scientific
sample, it is an interesting coincidence.

A characteristic of all three was the incorporation into their
behavior of an attitude of acceptance. I never saw them "take
someone down," whether to that person's face or, worse, behind
their back. People are people was their view, with no one perfect.
If we are all flawed, no one should carp at others' shortcomings.

One of my character defects has been a tendency to criticize
others. This trait was enhanced by my father's example and abetted
by my adopting the use of teasing as a teaching device. In learning
critical thinking, I found I could articulate what was wrong with
others or their poetry in a prioritized list replete with technical
terms. Years of spiritual training, fortunately, have helped me
become less judgmental. Squire Allworthy's example still inspires
me.

In your WJ assess how well you keep yourself from judging others.

Olding-Versus-Eldering Wisdom

Elders serve as conduits between the divine realm and the mundane world, making the abstract truths of spirituality accessible to the community by embodying them in their everyday behavior.
– Reb Zalman Schachter-Shalomi (1924–2014), *From Age-Ing to Sage-Ing*, 1995

Each year my wife and I join a dwindling group of friends, her old Earth Song shamanic-ritual buddies, to dance the Summer Solstice in at an 8,200-foot-high private retreat in the Rocky Mountains near Estes Park, Colorado.

A veteran of this annual rite is an 87-year-old master clock repairer named David, who this year hiked in, or I should say, *up* the four-and-a-half miles from the parking lot on U.S. 36. When he arrived and found no one there—the rest of us came an hour or so later—he started hiking down until the first of the later-arrivers picked him up and drove him back to camp.

At our initial sharing, before we opened the directions and started to dance, David made a distinction between what he called "olding," the creep of chronological age with its concomitant breaking down of the body and its once-smooth functioning, and "eldering." The first, he explained, is to a greater or lesser extent inevitable; the second requires ongoing attention to and work on oneself. The last clock-repair expert in Boulder, David still makes a half dozen or more "house-calls" each month, since it would take a village to move a grandfather clock to his shop. Although his body is still strong, he has also become a true wise elder as described by Reb Zalman above.

Write in your WJ about an elder you know and respect.

One-Percent Wisdom

Wealth consists not in having great possessions, but in having few wants.

— Epictetus (c. 55–c. 135)

In the fall of 2011 the Occupy Wall Street Movement created the slogan "We are the 99%." The top one percent of the population— net assets of at least $7,880,400 in 2013 (demos.org)—were, according to popular opinion, an elite minority of oligarchs who bought governments, enjoyed a luxurious life, and in effect ran the country and the world. Just ask 2016 presidential hopeful Bernie Sanders!

A decade ago I had a colleague who I believe was a member of that elite group. He seemed to have everything: a great professional life, a mansion of a house, a lovely wife and family, and the biggest Mercedes Benz I'd ever seen. He was also a nice, good-looking man from a distinguished family, was religious, played classical piano at a near-professional level, and was charitable. Yet one day his son committed suicide, and several years later my friend died of an apparent broken heart. So much for all his wealth.

Membership in the One-Percent club hardly guarantees happiness. True wealth has little to do with bank accounts, fancy cars, mansions, and the like. Rather, it is achieved through meaningful work, good families, healthy bodies, sound minds, and solid relationships with others. The members of this elite group are loving, deal well with adversity, search for meaning, and work for the common good, not just their own. Finally and happily, they are grateful for what they have rather than complain about all the things they lack.

Discuss in your WJ how you are striving for true wealth in your life.

Opportunity-Making Wisdom

A wise man will make more opportunities than he finds.
— Francis Bacon (1561–1626)

We are such an input-driven society. Before we go into business, we buy all kinds of equipment and supplies. We must be prepared for any business that comes our way. But the real art is finding a niche, an opportunity to attract customers, and provide the goods or services they want or need. We must create a business, not an office.

Similarly, there are people with state-of-the-art kitchens and everything in their fridge. Yet they can't cook, and their meals are hardly edible. Conversely, some people with little by way of equipment and supplies can serve up a feast by considering what's possible to create from what is at hand. Their creativity makes up for their lack of materials or tools. As the Italian composer Rossini is rumored to have said, "Give me a laundry list, and I will write you a beautiful opera."

Per Harry Truman, "A pessimist is one who makes difficulties of his opportunities and an optimist is one who makes opportunities of his difficulties." An inspiring example is Viktor Frankl, as noted in another essay in this book, who turned a concentration camp into a learning lab and a place to continue his development.

On a small scale, each of us can keep a paperback in our pocket to while away our waiting time in lines or learn to do mindful meditation while stuck in traffic. To the wise there are no bad times, only different kinds of opportunities.

In your WJ write about an occasion when you turned an unpromising situation into an opportunity.

Papal Wisdom

We must restore hope to young people, help the old, be open to the future, spread love. Be poor among the poor. We need to include the excluded and preach peace.

– Pope Francis I

When Jorge Mario Bergoglio, S.J., Cardinal of Buenos Aires, became the 266th Roman Catholic Pope on March 13th, 2013, he was the first ever Bishop of Rome from the New World. He was also the first Jesuit to be named head of the Catholic Church.

This last fact struck many as significant when he chose to name himself not Ignatius, after the soldier founder of his own order, but Francis, after the rich-kid-turned-hippy-preacher who talked with animals and founded the order of friars, the Franciscans. Here he was a first too: Francis I.

Although the leader of 1.2 billion Catholics, he has used his power wisely. A role model of humility, he has been guided by Matthew 7:1, "Judge not, lest you be judged." When asked early in his papacy about homosexuality, a condition condemned by his Church, he famously responded, "If a person is gay and seeks out the Lord and is willing, who am I to judge that person?" Later, when he was asked to explain himself, he said, "... People should not be defined only by their sexual tendencies: let us not forget that God loves all his creatures and we are destined to receive his infinite love."

Now 81 (born December 17, 1936), may he succeed in his effort to update his church. Too bad he can't be leader of *all* Christians.

In your WJ write what you think about this Pope.

Pastoral Wisdom

The Lord opened unto me that being bred at Oxford or Cambridge was not enough to fit and qualify men to be ministers of Christ.
— George Fox (1624–1691)

Pendulums swing back and forth. The first ministers of the Christian church, with the notable exception of Saint Paul, were simple people. But the time came when the public and church officials began to call for an "educated clergy." Oxford and Cambridge Universities began as monasteries. Monks more than priests represented the lettered and learned class of medieval Christendom. After the Reformation, the Anglican church preferred its clergy to be educated. Later, the New England Puritans shared that preference. Both Harvard and Yale were founded as places where, per Cotton Mather, "a succession of a learned and able ministry might be educated."

George Fox, the founder of the Quakers, understood that revelation, to be transformative, could not be a secondhand experience. With externally acquired knowledge, he believed, we would see through a glass darkly, not face-to-face.

Come to think of it, where did Jesus study? A carpenter's stepson, at 12 he was teaching the rabbis in the Temple. His learning seemed to come through such experiences as his 40-day fast in the desert. What seminary degree certified him to both speak and act with authority?

As a triple graduate of Yale, I am certainly grateful for my formal education. Yet I agree with George Fox that transformative education about divinity has to come from elsewhere. Pastoral wisdom is realizing that book learning alone is not sufficient to qualify one to shepherd God's people toward their Creator.

Write in your WJ about your spiritual formation.

Peaceful Wisdom

Let there be peace on earth and let it begin with me.
– From *Let There Be Peace on Earth* by Sy Miller and Jill Jackson
Miller, 1993

What can be wiser than learning to live in peace? Yet getting there has continued to be a big stretch for humankind. In John 14:27, Jesus' parting words to his followers are, "Peace I leave with you; My peace I give to you. I do not give to you as the world gives. Do not let your hearts be troubled; do not be afraid."

Peace in short is a gift to be received, not a prize to be won. Yet we have to prepare a place within where peace can land. And, as the Millers' song suggests, peacefulness begins with each one of us.

According to a saying of the Buddha (*Dhammapada*, Ch. 1), "If we face the fact of death, our quarrels will come to an end." In other words, recognizing that we are finite beings who will ultimately die, we will more likely be at peace with both ourselves and our neighbors.

In the verse just prior to the one in John's Gospel quoted above, Jesus says something else pertinent to this discussion: "But the Advocate, the Holy Spirit, whom the Father will send in My name, will teach you all things and will remind you of everything I have told you" (John 14:26). As I have emphasized throughout this book, wisdom and now its first cousin peace, though properties of the heart and mind, ultimately result from the Universal Spirit transforming us from within.

Discuss in your WJ how peaceful you are.

Perceptive Wisdom

The world you see is less of an indication about the world
and more of an indication about the vision you are using.

– Alan Cohen

We see what we are able to see. But we also see because of who we are. To a great extent, the eye is the I. Animals know this fact, for they look us directly in the eye. They are aware that this is somehow who we are and where we live.

We all see the same reality, people say. But do we? "I can't see it" is another way of saying "I don't get it," or "I don't understand." "I hear you" means the opposite. By taking the sentence "God is nowhere" and adding one space between the "w" and the "h" of "nowhere," you come up with "God is now here." The letters are exactly the same, but the meaning is the exact opposite. Everything depends on how we see things.

Sometimes it becomes necessary to look away in order to see something. This phenomenon happens to me regularly when I am doing crossword puzzles. If I can't find the right word, I set the puzzle aside for a while. When I return an hour or two later, *voilà!* The solution is obvious: my perception had changed in the interim.

In matters of greater import, unless the necessary wisdom is inside us, we may look but not see, listen but not understand. From this paradox we can conclude that perception is as much spiritual as physical. See?

Discuss in your WJ an example of seeing something in a new light. What conclusions would you draw?

Pilgrim Wisdom

Pilgrims are a hardy breed. They trudge rough roads, put in long days, and live on bread crusts... [And] on clear nights the stars that steer them cover them with their canopy and token the eternal.
– Huston Smith, Foreword to Phil Cousineau, *The Art of Pilgrimage*, 1998

For many secular Americans, *pilgrim* denotes one of the English Puritans who landed at Plymouth Rock in 1620. It may also bring to mind the struggle with our puritanical tendencies.

For Catholics, a pilgrim is likely someone traveling for spiritual renewal to Fatima, Lourdes, Santiago de Compostela, or Rome. Geoffrey Chaucer in *The Canterbury Tales* told how each April English people of all social classes would walk to Canterbury to pray at the tomb of Saint Thomas à Becket, the martyred cleric who put loyalty to church above loyalty to king (Henry II).

The concept of pilgrimage is common in many religions. Chinese worshipers climb many steps to Buddhist shrines. Hindus seek out the sacred city of Varanasi (formerly Benares). Jews attempt to visit the Holy Land to pray at the Wailing Wall. Muslims go on *hajj* to Mecca.

Fortunate are those whose life's walk seems meaningful to them. We might follow author-adventurer Phil Cousineau's lead in considering all travel as sacred pilgrimages. In the Introduction to his book he states, "What matters most on your journey is how deeply you see, how attentively you hear, how richly the encounters are felt in your heart and soul."

Do you have a sense of pilgrimage in your life? In your WJ sketch out where you have been and where you think you're headed.

Poetic Wisdom

Everywhere we are told that our human resources are all to be used... the inventions, the histories, every scrap of fact. But there is one kind of knowledge — infinitely precious, time-resistant... here to be passed between the generations... and that is poetry.
— Muriel Rukeyser (1913–1980), *The Life of Poetry*, 1949

My parents were not pleased by my decision to become a college English teacher. They were proud of my grades and academic honors, but I knew they were thinking, "A Phi Beta Kappa from Yale! He could do better." As children of poor immigrants, survivors of the Great Depression, and believers in the dollars-and-cents version of the American Dream, they couldn't understand my refusal to capitalize on my four-star education and enter a high-paying field.

Where were my riches? Well, passed between the generations there was, for example, this Wordsworth poem which I memorized in 1957 and still know today:

A slumber did my spirit seal,
I had no human fears:
She seemed a thing that could not feel
The touch of earthly years.

No motion has she now, no force;
She neither hears nor sees;
Rolled round in earth's diurnal course,
With rocks, and stones, and trees.

Even as a college student, I knew I would one day lose people I loved. Living presences would be no more. Then, like the poet, I would be forced to face the stony reality of death — but would be comforted by having first visited that place in living lines of verse.

In your WJ write about an especially meaningful poem and why it moves you.

Prayer Wisdom

There will always be prayers in public schools — as long as there are final exams to take.
— B. Norman Frisch, quoted in *The Complete Book of Practical Proverbs and Wacky Wit*, 1996

I was good at school. So I never prayed before exams. On the other hand, I did pray before swim meets. As my team's third starter in my event, I usually asked for at least a third. Mostly I came in fourth or fifth. My prayers were regular, just not effective.

As an adult, I pray more frequently, even before walking or running. I usually ask that my body be protected, especially my knees, legs, feet, and back. I also remember to warm up and cool down, since prayer shouldn't be a substitute for doing my part. Maybe the problem with my swimming prayers at prep school was that I never trained hard enough or didn't have the right stuff to begin with. Maybe some of our prayers are answered by not being answered, at least not as we hope.

A friend experiencing hard times told me of a breakthrough she'd had. Having prayed for what she considered positive outcomes, she spontaneously requested the strength and understanding to accept however God wanted her situations to end. She surrendered her desires and expectations to the Universe. Then, for the first time since the start of her hard times, she felt a new sense of freedom. Several days later things turned out exactly as she had hoped. She sat on the floor of her apartment and wept. All the Universe wanted, it seemed, was for her to let go.

In your WJ discuss your prayer life.

Primal Wisdom

Today, as technocratic society falters on the brink of the cliff of its own making, many members of our society... [are] searching their souls for spiritual and mystical guidance in the wasteland of materialism.
— Robin Clarke and Geoffrey Hindley, *The Challenge of the Primitives*, 1975

The concept of the Noble Savage appeared just as the Industrial Revolution was picking up steam. Former peasants were crowding into Manchester and London to work long hours in the polluted, unsafe factories of the late-eighteenth and early-nineteenth centuries. Although there was still enough countryside to inspire Wordsworth, Coleridge, and the Lake Poets, Dickens' novels of urban blight and exploitation would be eagerly read in serialized form in the nation's periodicals.

It is tempting to romanticize country living in general and primal societies in particular. Thoreau was right to note rural as well as urban despair. Today middle-aged farmers have one of America's highest suicide rates. Meanwhile huge urban areas are springing up like mushrooms in less developed countries as peasants are leaving their farms and rural homes for the lure of jobs in the city.

The British anthropologists quoted above do have a point. People linked through commonly understood traditions and the belief that all things are endued with spirit tend to live with greater respect for one another and their environment. They reinforce each other in the conviction that without community they cannot survive. Perhaps Wisdom is now calling us to adapt the spirit-filled ethic of primal peoples to meet the needs of our overly individualistic postindustrial society.

Discuss in your WJ several lessons you think primal cultures have for us today.

Progress-Versus-Perfection Wisdom

Most of our failings are habits we have allowed ourselves to form and keep. We will probably never be perfect, but we can be less imperfect.

– The Twelve Steps and Twelve Traditions of the Al-Anon Groups, 1980

I joined Al-Anon in 1992 so that I could help a recovering alcoholic in my family. Before long I also discovered that I had areas in my life that had not yet been reached by my other self-development regimens. By using the tools of the Twelve Step programs, I was slowly but surely helping to craft a better and wiser me.

One of the great psychological insights of Twelve Step programs is that the call to personal perfection can be deadly. Our parents require us as children to toe various lines—to think this way, dress like that, play with those kids, have these values, prepare for this profession. As the psychiatrist and author M. Scott Peck, MD, pointed out in his *The Road Less Traveled* (1978), but for overly demanding and other types of dysfunctional parents, he and his fellow psychotherapists would have little or no clientele.

Perfection sets the bar so high that we can never clear it. No one is quite so critical as we are when we get on our own case and strive for self-perfection. The Al-Anon insight is that the drive to perfection only sets us up for failure. The phrase you hear at meetings is "progress not perfection." This garden-variety piece of wisdom is one of the reasons Twelve Step programs have helped so many people including me.

Write in your WJ how you deal with your perfectionist tendencies.

Right-Use-of-Power Wisdom

Ethics is simply the right use of power.
– Amina Knowlan, Founder of Matrix Leadership

My wife, Cedar Barstow, is a psychotherapist. Some years ago, when she was directing the institute associated with her brand of therapy, she was asked to create an ethics program for therapists in training. After reviewing lists of dos and don'ts, she decided that ethics went beyond memorizing such lists. Her colleague, Amina, suggested it was really a matter of learning to use one's personal and role power well. Ethics, Amina thought, was the right use of one's power.

Today Cedar is executive director of the Right Use of Power Institute (RUPI), a nonprofit in Boulder, Colorado. Thousands have been trained to use their power more effectively by some 280 program teachers worldwide. Thousands more have read Cedar's two books on the subject, listened to a webinar, or earned related continuing-education units.

Cedar talks about the power differential between up-power and down-power people. These differences must be recognized and responded to. We need to stand in our power while staying in our hearts. That means learning to avoid the extremes of being dictators or doormats and finding just the right way to use our power in every situation. We need to regard the impact of our words and deeds more than our intentions. We must come to admit our interpersonal mistakes and learn to make effective apologies. Appropriate uses of power are essential in all personal, organizational, even international relations. Now more than ever, we all need to use our power wisely and well.

How do you tend to use your power? Do a mini-self-analysis in your WJ.

Sabbath Wisdom

Some keep the Sabbath going to church;
I keep it staying at home,
With a bobolink for a chorister,
And an orchard for a dome...

God preaches, —a noted clergyman, —
And the sermon is never long;
So instead of getting to heaven at last,
I'm going all along!

– Emily Dickinson (1830–1886)*

My wife and I are regular churchgoers. We appreciate many aspects of institutional church life, from the services themselves to adult-education opportunities to men's and women's groups. Our sanctuary is beautiful, and our chapel in the round is used for all kinds of special services. The choir, which contains many professional singers, is led by a locally renowned conductor, and our organist is a composer and virtuoso player. Best of all are our priests and deacons, especially our female rector, but all are excellent if in different ways.

Nevertheless, to tell the truth, I agree with Emily Dickinson that God's house is bigger than any formal place of worship. Not everyone who follows the rules of his or her religion necessarily keeps the Sabbath in a real sense, while some who never set foot inside a house of worship live in intimacy with God. There is no easy way to tell.

God's world, I believe, is much more inclusive than ours. Who forbids a sunset or a rainbow on grounds of some formal affiliation? Capitalists and communists alike may listen to a nightingale without visas or special permits. God seems very willing to meet individuals where they are. Shouldn't we do the same?

Write in your WJ about your sabbath-day practice or your reasons for not having one.

Sailing Wisdom

Tomorrow we again embark upon the boundless sea.
– Horace (65–8 BCE), Odes, I, VII 32

Viewed from the moon, the earth is covered with a single body of water. The division between Atlantic and Pacific is an invisible line running from the Tierra del Fuego at the bottom of Argentina to Antarctica. On one side is the Atlantic; on the other, the Pacific. Waves keep trying to erase this arbitrary boundary, but our mapmakers, representing civilization, keep drawing them back in.

Though "boundless," the sea is full of places to land. Harbors abound in the boundless sea. Sailors all, we awaken each day and embark on our renewed journey through life. In nautical lingo, we are all simply day sailors.

Horace's line can also be understood negatively. If the sea is indeed boundless, there are no ports to be had. Each day we sail out and return, regardless of wind and weather, with no real destination in mind.

As a sailor, however, I can state that no two trips are ever alike. Wind, weather, current, and boat weight change everything. New experiences foster new skills. Remembering similar situations, we respond with increased competence and confidence. Because we have no set destination, every day provides fresh opportunities to experience new vistas. Who knows? One day we may sail beyond the horizon and, like Columbus, discover new worlds.

When you wake up tomorrow, go outside, greet the morning, and ask for a blessing on the day trip on which you are about to embark. Before going to sleep at night, write briefly in your WJ about the significant experiences of the "day-sail" just completed.

Saintly Wisdom

Voices, voices. Listen, my heart, as only
Saints once listened. When the gigantic Call
Raised them off the floor, they, the Impossible Ones,
Kept right on kneeling and didn't even notice.
That's how much they were listening.
       – Rainer Maria Rilke (1875–1926), from the "First Duino
       Elegy" (coauthor's translation)

Saintly wisdom is not about knowledge but behavior. The story of Satan and his rebellious angels highlights a chief characteristic of angels and saints: obedience. To hear is to obey. They listen to God's voice and follow orders. Guardian angels whisper in our ear when we are about to go off track. They may just be that "still, small voice" usually ascribed to our conscience.

Saints know enough to listen to God's voice and follow. For most of us, it's not so easy. We hear lots of voices. How do we pick one and do the right thing? History is full of false messiahs who led themselves and others astray.

Jesus showed us how to listen. He prayed for guidance in the Garden of Gethsemane just before his arrest. As our human brother, he said, in effect, "Look, I would just as soon not die, especially in this way." Then he added what I call The Great Nevertheless: "Father, if it be your will, remove this cup from me; nevertheless, not my will, but your will be done" (Luke 22:42).

The way of saintly wisdom is learning to listen to and follow not self-will, peer pressure, or current fashion, but that still, small voice within.

How well do you hear and follow your still, small voice? Share an example or two in your WJ.

Scriptural Wisdom

All Scripture is inspired by God and is useful for teaching the truth, rebuking error, correcting faults, and giving instruction for right living, so that the person who serves God may be fully qualified and equipped to do every kind of good deed.

— 2 Timothy 3:16–17 (*Good News Bible*, 2nd ed.)

Soon after moving to Hawaii in 1967, I began attending Church of the Crossroads, a United Church of Christ congregation near the university. The minister was a charismatic preacher with strong left-wing leanings that made him controversial. The services were rarely boring.

One feature of Crossroads' services was the reading of the Scriptures. Whereas most churches have Old and New Testament readings, Crossroads had Old, New, and *Now* Testament ones. This very 60s concept still makes sense to me.

If *this* book of mini-essays is about anything, it is the universality of wisdom. Since God created everything, everything contains its maker's signature. And God's signature is *Wisdom*. As Jesus so often said, we need have only the eyes to see and the ears to hear. Wisdom is within each of us—our neighbors, even our enemies.

What then is "Scripture"? For me, whatever leads me closer to God's will for my life is Scripture. It need not be Jewish or Christian or even something I understand with my conscious mind. Nor need it be "religious." The poetry of Rilke, Matthias Claudius, and Wordsworth form part of my Scripture. So do the "Big Book" of Alcoholics Anonymous, Frankl's *Man's Search for Meaning*, and Gibran's *The Prophet*. What about you?

In your WJ talk about a few non-biblical works that comprise your Scripture.

Self-Healing Wisdom

A man's own observation, what he finds good of and what he finds hurt of, is the best physic to preserve health.
— Francis Bacon (1561–1626)

In Bacon's time, medical care was quite different from what we have today. Physicians in the Elizabethan period administered a physic typically some form of herbal remedy. St. Hildegard of Bingen (1098–1179), the German abbess and mystic, was well known in twelfth-century Europe as an herbalist and healer. Elizabethans also believed that imbalances in the blood caused illness and could be corrected by using leeches to draw the bad blood out. Doctors were thus called "leeches" back then.

In a time when people made their own soap, clothes, and even shoes, the idea of being one's own physician was not far-fetched. Folk cures and family remedies abounded. But Bacon, an early scientist and pragmatist, advised readers not to depend on generally accepted remedies, whether from doctors or neighborhood wisdom. We should see what works for us. If something makes us feel better, we should continue it. If not, we should try something else.

In our era of modern medicine, we tend to call on specialists in their fields. In so doing we have given away much of the freedom to heal ourselves. "In-tuition," as Gloria Steinem points out in her 1992 book *Revolution from Within*, means an inner capacity to teach ourselves. An important wisdom way is thus recovering an intuitive, reality-based sense of what is good for our bodies and what is not and then living accordingly.

Do you practice healing yourself? How well do you listen to, then treat, your body? Respond in your WJ.

Self-Help Wisdom

The gods help those who help themselves.
– Aesop (c. 620–564 BCE), "Hercules and the Waggoner,"
c. 550 BCE

This is a saying we self-reliant Americans love. We are, after all, a society of rugged individualists. Entrepreneurship and innovation are our life's blood. We like to help ourselves—to figure out what's wrong with our bodies, minds, spirits, or pocketbooks; then adopt a regimen to help us do better. These programs, if we stick with them, often work.

Benjamin Franklin created a plan for successful living. Basically, you spend one week concentrating on one of thirteen virtues. You observe how you are doing in that week's virtue, be it silence, industry, or moderation. Then you move on to the next. You go through four cycles each year as you assess and improve your practice of each virtue.

This program presumably helped Franklin, the tenth child of a poor, obscure Bostonian, become one of the most affluent individuals in the Colonies. He could retire early from self-employment—two other American ideals—and devote himself entirely to public service, a third. His civic good works form a long list that includes founding a hospital, a university, the U.S. Postal Service, and the U.S. Mint. Not bad results for a self-help disciple!

Not every self-help program, however, is effective for everyone. To borrow a saying from the Twelve Step community, you have to work your own program. Still, much can be said for those that succeed, something we each need to learn for ourselves.

Describe in your WJ a success or failure you've had with a self-help program. What lessons did you draw from the experience?

Shakertown Wisdom

I make the following declarations: I am a world citizen. I commit myself to lead an ecologically sound life; to lead a life of creative simplicity and to share my personal wealth with the world's poor; to join with others in reshaping institutions in order to bring about a more just global society; to avoid the creation of products that cause harm; to care for my physical well-being, affirming that my body is a gift; to examine continually my relations with others; to personal renewal through prayer, meditation, and study; to responsible participation in a community of faith.

– The Shakertown Pledge, 1973

It may be a gift to be simple, but no one said it would be easy. To think that I attended fifteen retreats at the actual restored Shaker village where this pledge was crafted. And no wonder!

Shakertown was the right place to develop such a pledge. Although the last Shaker there died before World War I, the community at Pleasant Hill, Kentucky, was restored and is now an interpretive museum with a guest house, a restaurant, two gift shops, and conference facilities for small groups. The Shaker spirit of spare, functional beauty is palpable everywhere.

If the Shakertown Pledge were taken and followed by even a minority of the developed world's population, the impact in the new millennium would be, well, millennial. My sense is that whether we know it or not, we are all being moved in this direction. What do you think?

Which of the Shakertown commitments might you commit to and what effect do you think that action would have on your life? Respond in your WJ.

Simple-Gifts Wisdom

*When the solution is simple, God is answering... Things should be
as simple as possible, but not any simpler.*
– Albert Einstein (1879–1955)

We are taught that knowledge and sophistication are good. When I
was twenty, a newly minted Yale graduate, I was at the height of my
sophistication which, in my case, was a first cousin to arrogance.

Graduate school cured me of my smugness. As an
undergraduate I had been a star. Yale graduate school was another
matter. My new colleagues knew as much as I did—or more. One
significant incident occurred during my first year in the English
Ph.D. program, when I attended a lecture by Dr. René Wellek, the
then Sterling Professor of Comparative Literature.

In a brilliant performance he demonstrated a broad and
deep knowledge of the languages and literatures of a half dozen
countries. I realized with depressing clarity that I would never
know as much as Professor Wellek nor be able to give a lecture
like the one I'd just heard. In that mood I returned to my shared
student digs, opened the third-floor window, and put one leg
out with the intention to jump. Fortunately, I didn't. I made it
through graduate school and got my doctorate five years later. But
that incident marked the end of my intellectual snobbery and the
beginning of a process of simplification that continues to this day.

When all the gifts are counted, surely one of the greatest, as
Einstein suggested, will be simplicity.

*Do you live as simply as possible? Write in your WJ how you might
simplify yourself and your life even further.*

Solomon's Wisdom

For the Lord bestows wisdom and teaches knowledge and understanding.

– Proverbs 2:6

What is wisdom? "Knowledge of what is true or right coupled with good judgment," says one dictionary. Another adds that this good judgment is about "action." The Anglo-Saxon roots are *wis* and *deman*: to make judgments ("to deem" in modern English) based on knowledge or understanding (cp. *wissen*: "to know" in German).

Solomon's famous judgment (1 Kings 3) exemplifies wisdom in this sense. Two women, prostitutes living in the same house, asked the king to settle their dispute. One asserted that the other had suffocated her child by accident while asleep. On waking she allegedly had substituted her dead infant for the living child of her house-mate. The second woman insisted the living child was hers.

Solomon called for a sword, commanded that the child be cut into two pieces, and ruled that each woman should be given an equal share. One demanded her half. The other protested, "Give the whole child to her!" Solomon reasoned that the real mother would prefer losing a living child to receiving half of a dead one. So, based on this understanding, he gave the child to the woman who had protested.

Solomon is the Bible's poster-child for wisdom. When we learn, however, that he had 700 wives and 300 concubines (1 Kings 11) and that he got into trouble with God over one wife in particular, we may wonder just how wise Solomon really was.

What do you think wisdom is? Compose a definition in your WJ. Do you think your own wisdom has increased by reading this book? Why or why not?

Soul Wisdom

When you have shut your doors and darkened your room, remember... you are not alone; but God is within, and your genius is within, and what need have they of light to see what you are doing?

– Epictetus (c. 55–c. 135)

An abiding theological quest is to decide on the transcendence or immanence of divinity. Is God out there or in here? Some traditions, like Deism, have reduced God to a distant creator, a kind of absentee parent who started life, then left it to its own devices. The image often used is the divine clockmaker.

Traditions like Judaism and Islam posit a more involved deity. Jehovah and Allah create, guide, lay down rules for, and punish or reward their creatures. God is nevertheless still above and beyond us. Mystical traditions, on the other hand, understand God as a force pervading the universe and living within each creature. According to mystics, human beings need to become aware of and eventually attain union with the God within, that is, our souls.

Unfortunately, the inner and outer aspects of religion have historically had a somewhat tense relationship. Established communities, based on broadly accepted and sanctioned tenets of faith, are understandably concerned about mystical freelancers.

As in most matters, the middle way seems best. God is both out there—the Supreme Other—and in here—our souls. To follow the ethical tenets of one's faith is a good idea. Meanwhile, to live in accordance with the promptings of God from within will assure, as the song suggests, that we will never walk alone.

Discuss in your WJ how you experience your soul.

Sound-Priorities Wisdom

Beloved Pan... give me beauty in the inward soul; and may the outward and inward man [sic] be as one. May... I have such a quantity of gold as none but the temperate can carry.
— Plato (c. 427–347 BCE), *Phaedrus*

The first priority here is that we are limited beings who may get life wrong and may not realize this fact until too late. Faith in powers higher and wiser than ourselves is thus an immense gift.

Next comes understanding and accepting that our essential self is more important than our personality. The former refers to that part of us that will continue after death; the latter to our equipment for living here. Being overly concerned with the outer aspects of life distracts us from pursuing those activities that have a deeper meaning.

The priority that follows is integrating our inner and outer selves. Integration leads to integrity. Wearing a mask that belies who and what we are causes us, literally, to be hypocrites, from the Greek word for actors, people who wear masks and pretend to be someone or something they are not. Working on ourselves has the goal of bringing the inner and outer person, our essence and personality, together.

Finally, one must understand that true riches, like the Kingdom of Heaven, lie within. We must have only as much material wealth as we can carry without it going to our heads. We should consider wisdom the true coin of the realm.

What are your life priorities? Where does the integration of inner and outer self fall on your list? Please answer in your WJ.

Steady Wisdom

One who is not disturbed in mind even amidst the threefold miseries or elated when there is happiness and who is free from attachment, fear, and anger is called a sage of steady mind.
– Bhagavad-Gita, Prabhupada Translation

When I graduated from college in 1960, *meditate* to me meant "thinking hard about something over time." My image was Rodin's great sculpture *The Thinker*, an individual bent over, his head in his hand.

The next year I met Kasi, a South Indian Brahmin working on a doctorate in accounting at Northwestern University. I was between undergraduate and grad school and was spending the year at my parents' apartment in Chicago. Kasi helped me understand that the sculpture I should have had in mind for Eastern meditation was the contemplative Buddha. Kasi also took me to the Vivekananda Vedanta Center, not three blocks from where I was living, to experience the thing itself.

I remember sitting in that quiet room on Elm Street, trying not to think of anything. Of course, I couldn't. It was always easier when Swami Vishwananda arrived and began intoning in basso Sanskrit. His words translated to "Bring us from the unreal to the Real."

Soon I learned about the classical Hindu concept of the wise person who was trained to avoid radical mood swings. As a tortoise draws in its legs, so the person of steady wisdom withdraws into the quiet shell of meditation and learns to act without attachment to the results.

In your WJ write about your experience of meditation. Otherwise, sit quietly and for 20 minutes let your thoughts come and go. Then, write about the experience.

Stewardship Wisdom

In the Judeo-Christian tradition, the biblical concept of dominion is quite different from the concept of domination, and the difference is crucial. Specifically, followers of this tradition are charged with the duty of stewardship, because the same biblical passage that grants them "dominion" also requires them to "care for" the earth even as they "work" it.

– Al Gore, Earth in the Balance, 1993

Many of my experiences of the 1960s took place during my time teaching at the University of Hawaii. In those days Hawaii seemed five years behind the mainland in everything. The first campus protest didn't take place till 1968: a sit-in at the administration building over what was considered the unwarranted firing of a political-science professor.

Besides students, a sprinkling of faculty participated. Interestingly, many were idealistic untenured assistant professors—the very ones with the most to lose. The "enemy" consisted of the president and the Board of Regents, political appointees whose concept of stewardship, it appeared, had more to do with domination than dominion.

One of my friends back then pointed out how we in the Western world impale our food with forks and cut it with knives, while East Asians use wooden chopsticks, and the nations of South and Southeast Asia traditionally eat gently with their hands. As theologian Diana Butler Bass pointed out in 2015, the verb *soil* means to dirty, smudge, mar. How could we possibly respect the earth?

I have less trouble now with the dominion concept so long as we are talking about good, caring management. Domination, however, should never be confused with stewardship.

In your WJ discuss what you mean by "stewardship."

Storytelling Wisdom

Hidden in all stories is the One story... In telling them, we are telling each other the human story. Stories that touch us in this place of common humanness awaken us and weave us together as a family once again... Facts bring us to knowledge, but stories lead to wisdom.
— Rachel Naomi Remen, M.D., *Kitchen Table Wisdom*, 1996

When I began writing this book, people sent me quotations, proverbs, ideas, even stories. Still, I was surprised when Dr. Remen's book, quoted above, arrived in the mail. It just showed up. No bill, no gift card, nothing.

When I was five, we lived in Great Neck, Long Island, a New York City suburb. Every Saturday morning my parents would drive me to the local public library, where a nice woman would read us stories. My favorite was *Winnie-the-Pooh*. I remember being intrigued by the quirky animals and their quaint way of speaking. Those and other stories both touched me and opened something inside me. Still, those Saturday-morning storytelling sessions had an unexpectedly negative effect on me: I was slow to learn to read and preferred being read to. There was something about the voice and presence of another person.

Moral: Our all-too-human tendencies to gossip or criticize should be put on hold. Instead, we should share ourselves and our experiences with others through story. For while criticism excludes, stories include. When we study the lives and cultures of humankind, their stories really can lead to wisdom.

In your WJ write about your favorite childhood story. Why do you think this particular story appealed to you?

Studious Wisdom

What else therefore do we do when we study to be wise except to concentrate our whole soul with all the ardor we can upon what we touch with our mind, and as it were place it there and fix it unshakeably?

— Saint Augustine of Hippo (354–430), *On Free Choice*

If you were planning a workshop on "Enhancing Your Personal Wisdom," you could be forgiven for asking, "What does Augustine mean, and how do I apply his advice in my daily life?" His philosophical language, at least as translated here, is daunting.

Fortunately, it is often possible to sort through such abstract passages for meaning. This essay by Augustine is on free choice. Here he implies that we are each free to seek wisdom or not. If wisdom becomes our goal, we must look for it with all our strength in everything we do. Wisdom is all around us, but to see and acquire it, we have to become lifelong students and transformers of abstract thought into concrete action.

We must do our looking, however, without entangling ourselves in webs of differences. A banana is not a tomato, yet both are fruits. A cosmic ray is not the morning newspaper, yet both consist of energy. A human being is not a gecko, yet both are creatures. Jesus' advice that by seeking we shall find is appropriate here. Seeing God in or behind all things regardless of their apparent differences is both goal and path. Our job is to walk Augustine's talk.

In your WJ describe a practical exercise you might use if you were giving a wisdom workshop.

Teacher Wisdom

If... [the teacher] is indeed wise he [sic] does not bid you enter the house of his wisdom, but rather leads [you] to the threshold of your own mind.

– Kahlil Gibran, *The Prophet*, 1923

Wisdom, like the Kingdom of Heaven, lies within each of us. In many cases it's an undiscovered country, not yet on our maps. We may be afraid to set forth on our voyage of discovery, discontented with our old life but not yet ready for something else.

Alas, some teachers and parents force children to learn this or do that before their time. Then, if there's a family tradition of attending a particular college or entering a specific profession, the children better go there and become that. Family businesses often fail because the founder's only child, with little talent and less inclination, is forced to take over.

The wise teacher understands that each human being is his or her own school, his or her own temple. The teaching function is sacred and must be undertaken with due regard that wherever teaching/learning takes place is holy ground. It is not accidental that the Hebrew *rabbi* and Sanskrit *guru*, both spiritual terms, mean "teacher."

Whether, when, and how we learn are mysteries. Teachers can share knowledge and techniques with their students, but they are at their best and most impactful when they share themselves. Example along with experience is the best teacher. If students are given permission, they will be able to learn from and for themselves. They thus become their own teachers.

In your WJ recount an instance when you learned something significant "from yourself."

The Love Doctor's Wisdom

Each day we are offered new means for learning and growing in love... Even the most insignificant thing can bring us closer to ourselves and therefore to others.
        – Leo Buscaglia, Ph.D. (1924–1998), *Love*, 1972

Leo Buscaglia became well known as the Love Doctor in the seventies through his books and televised lectures. The former were sometimes offered as premiums during PBS pledge drives. After viewing one of his TV lectures, I was hooked. Making a pledge at the next opportunity, I requested his latest book as my prize.

A signature event after each in-person lecture was his hug line. Virtually every person in a large auditorium would queue up to receive a bear hug from the master.

But love for the Love Doctor meant more than hugs. He told the story of going to Europe without his Italian-immigrant mother's blessing. Apparently, she wanted him to finish his schooling first. Having some savings, he decided to go anyway and ended up in Paris. There he developed quite a circle by throwing parties, all of which he paid for from his quickly diminishing savings. Before he knew it, his funds had run out, and his friends all suddenly disappeared.

Sending the cheapest telegram possible, he wrote his mother: "Mama, Starving, Felice [his Italian first name]." The telegram she sent back was equally terse: "Felice, Starve, Mamma." He'd come face-to-face with "tough love." From that experience he learned about budgeting, listening to your elders, setting boundaries, and knowing who your real friends are.

Write for five minutes in your WJ about what you believe are the characteristics of genuine love.

The Wisdom of Acceptance

*Freedom consists in making the best of what we have, our parentage,
our physical nature and mental gifts. Every kind of capacity, every
form of vocation, if rightly used, will lead us to the centre.*
– Radhakrishnan (1888–1975), *The Hindu View of Life*

America is known as the land of opportunity. People continue to
immigrate here and make something of their lives. Once *Parade
Magazine* featured a Mexican-American family. They never earned
much, but with determination and hard work they made sure all
their many children graduated from college. One became a priest,
another a physician, two others correctional workers, and so on.
Each made it into the middle class.

Yet America is also a country where we are tempted to act more
important than we really are. A name change can create a Gatsby
from a Gatz. Plastic surgery can help one marry up, get a better job,
or pass for someone more attractive.

Surely there is wisdom in having high goals, working hard,
and giving life one's best shot. One can also give up before getting
started, a less productive approach to opportunity.

Radhakrishnan, the philosopher who became president of
India, is right. Our genetic makeup, the time and place of our
birth, and the quality of the parenting we receive are all limiting
factors over which we have no control. Yet only by accepting these
limitations can we work to overcome them and become all we have
the potential to be.

*Think about something in your makeup that has been a challenge for
you to accept. In your WJ write down three positive things about this
characteristic.*

The Wisdom of Asking Questions

I am Yours and born for You. What do You want of me?
                                    – St. Teresa of Avila (1515–1582)

Asking questions is fifty percent of finding answers. Maybe more. Science is built on asking good questions. Learning how to construct them is one of the main tasks, I would say, of an outstanding liberal education.

My dear friend the late Sister Eileen Rice, O.P., was, as she would say, the teacher-education department at Siena Heights College, a Dominican institution in Adrian, Michigan. And what a teacher she was! While interviewing her for a documentary about her life shortly before her death, I asked her about influences on her own formation as a teacher. She mentioned, among other things, the askers of "stunning" questions. She referred to those people as a kind of "anonymous Greek chorus" who after a lecture would come up with pointed, useful questions that would bring the discussion to a new level of clarity.

We self-sufficient moderns tend to answer more than we ask. Like so many radio-talk-show listeners, we prefer to call in and generously speak our minds rather than let the guest respond to a well-designed question. Teresa of Avila helps us understand that God is the source of our wisdom. It is best, therefore, to ask God for guidance as often as possible, to learn to discern the answers, and then to have the courage to follow what we have received.

Think of a question for your Higher Power and write it down in your WJ. Then meditate on it for ten minutes and record any answer you may have received in the quietness.

The Wisdom of Associating with Remarkable People

As a definition of who may be considered... remarkable, I will simply say... he can be called a remarkable man who stands out from those around him by the resourcefulness of his mind, and who knows how to be restrained in the manifestations that proceed from his nature, at the same time conducting himself justly and tolerantly towards the weakness of others.

– G.I. Gurdjieff (1877–1949), Meetings with Remarkable Men, 1963

I first encountered Gurdjieff's program for harmonious human development in 1960. A friend in a Gurdjieff group in Chicago began feeding me books. At first, I read those by some of his pupils. The most exciting was P.D. Ouspensky's *In Search of the Miraculous*. My friend said Gurdjieff's own books were so abstruse, they were best tackled after reading commentaries by his followers.

I didn't join a group but appreciated learning about Gurdjieff's distinction between "personality" (one's ego self) and "essence" (one's true inner nature). His goal of self-development was learning to identify with the latter. When I finally read Gurdjieff's *Meetings with Remarkable Men*, I was impressed that someone would be considered remarkable only to the extent that they impacted us as individuals. His list included his father, the village priest, and a retired Russian general, among others.

Although I never became a Gurdjieff follower, I believe his system served as a bridge between my intellectuality and my ability to follow a spiritual path. Thus he will always be remarkable for me.

In your WJ list several "remarkable" people in your life. Then speculate on why you chose them.

118

The Wisdom of Caring

We won't always know whose lives we touched and
made better for our having cared, because
actions can sometimes have unforeseen ramifications.
What's important is that you do care and you act.
— Charlotte Lunsford Berry

Not all popular movements are to be disdained. One not long ago, spread by bumper stickers, urged us to "practice random acts of kindness." The phrasing no doubt stemmed from the random acts of violence that had become the staple shock-fare of the nightly news. The advice was likely meant to counterbalance such negative deeds.

In Honolulu I once did some fundraising for the Visitor Aloha Society of Hawaii, or VASH, a nonprofit organization that does nice things for tourists who have become victims of crime. In coordination with the agency, which receives referrals from the police department, hotels offer free accommodations, restaurants provide free meals, nightclubs give free tickets to shows, and so on, to victims of local crime. The idea in the tourist-dependent 50th State is to make sure crime victims leave Hawaii with the memory that the Aloha Spirit has prevailed for them.

Acts of caring are like seeds that can take root and become fruitful in others. Ultimately people—especially the young or those in lower power positions—need good examples. What we do or say can impact our spouses, children, partners, students, customers, even strangers encountered once. Because it takes so little effort to be caring, it behooves us all to take noted philanthropist Charlotte Berry's words to heart and assimilate this wisdom into our daily living.

In your WJ describe the impact someone else's kindness has had on your life.

The Wisdom of Change

They must often change who would be constant in happiness or wisdom.

— Confucius (551–479 BCE)

Our situations change all the time. Sometimes we cause the change. More often, external factors are at work, and we need to respond appropriately. Different music, different dance.

Two issues immediately surface. One is our ability to hear the change in the music; the other is our familiarity with the new dance. Sometimes waiting is the best policy. We stay on the sidelines until the music changes to a dance we know. Or else we can ask someone to teach us the basic steps.

Since childhood I have heard different music and changed my dance often. I was always a good mimic and did well with foreign languages. Not only did I get the accents right, but people remarked that my facial expression and body language changed too. I began to wonder whether I had a central self that could act in different ways, or if I was simply a chameleon by nature. Who was I anyway?

Following my spiritual practice has, through time, helped me gain the sense of an inner self which does not change. However, my demeanor automatically adjusts to outward circumstances. When I am with young children, I play. When I am at a party, I dance. When I am in the library, I study. But I no longer feel that I lack an essential self just because my behavior changes to fit a new situation. I am the same dancer as before, just doing a different dance.

How do you adjust to changing situations? Discuss this question in your WJ.

The Wisdom of Divine Guidance

When looking back on the lives of men and women of God the tendency is to say—"What wonderfully astute wisdom they had!" ... We give credit to human wisdom when we should give credit to the Divine guidance of God.

> – Oswald Chambers (1874–1917), *My Utmost for His Highest*, 1935

True wisdom, according to Chambers, is an attribute of God. Human wisdom by itself is insufficient to stand up to the changes and chances of life. Those of us who assume that human wisdom is all we need for the good life will misconstrue the "men and women of God" as those who have mastered the art of life and have lived accordingly.

The human-centered idea of wisdom begins with our free will and a kind of tacit agreement with the Deity to leave us human beings to struggle our way to living in a positive manner. This view is the inverse of the theocentric concept. Here, human wisdom is our God-given capacity to handle whatever situation life may deal us. It is merely a question of whether we are innately wise or have learned from experience how to deal with life's challenges.

As a believer with a strong humanistic education, I think we should use our mind and will to deal with whatever confronts us. We shouldn't presume on God to do our work for us. But we should also be willing to "let go and let God." True wisdom, as the *Serenity Prayer* suggests, is knowing when to do which.

Write in your WJ how you sort out the conundrum of human wisdom and God's wisdom.

The Wisdom of Faith

God our Father has made all things depend on faith so that whoever has faith will have everything, and whoever does not have faith will have nothing.
– Martin Luther (1483–1546), *The Freedom of a Christian*, 1520

Luther was a lover of all-or-nothing statements. Ironically, this one found its way into an attempt to reconcile with Rome. Personal faith was basic to Luther's reform, which arrived in the world at roughly the same time as individualism and nationalism. A biblical scholar, translator, Augustinian monk, and Catholic priest, Luther knew that when Jesus healed people in the Gospel stories, he assigned credit either to the Father or to the individual's faith.

Centuries later in his book *The Laws of Spirit* (1995), Dan Millman wrote, "Faith is our direct link to universal wisdom, reminding us that we know more than we have heard or read or studied — that we have only to... trust the love and wisdom of the Universal Spirit working through us all."

Luther's statement on faith is stern, while Millman's reminds us that tolerance and optimism characterize modern human-development literature. Faith, per Millman, is recognizing that each of us contains the wisdom of the universe and the ability to get whatever we need from Universal Spirit.

Luther and Millman do agree on one thing: Faith is the key. Without it the most important doors of living will not be opened. It seems as though every person has the potential for linkage to a kind of cosmic Internet. Once faith activates that potential, we must use it.

How would you describe your faith? Write about it in your WJ.

The Wisdom of Giving and Receiving

The Sufi opens his hand to the universe and gives away each instant, free. Unlike someone who begs on the street for money to survive, a dervish begs to give you his life.
– Jalaluddin Rumi (1207–1273), Coleman Barks Translation

I was once development director for a nonprofit agency offering homeless people transitional shelter. It helped house, clothe, feed, and counsel such people while equipping them to support themselves.

From that experience I learned that not everyone on the streets is homeless, and not everyone in an apartment or house is accommodated. Among the former, some seem healthy-minded and optimistic enough to make it if given half a chance. Others seem wrecked from alcohol, drugs, mental illness, or other causes. More than a hand up, they seem to need a miraculous laying on of hands.

The gestures to give and to receive are really the same. In both cases, you put your hand out, palm up. The essential attitude, I suppose, is being open and available. A clenched fist can neither give nor receive.

Inner content is what differentiates a Sufi from a beggar. A beggar is simply needy. Having nothing, the latter feels like nothing. The Sufi, by contrast, receives in order to give, gives in order to receive. My own spiritual guide, from the Sufi tradition of Islamic spirituality, once said that wells that give themselves away stay pure, while boarded-up wells soon become polluted from the lack of replenishment and circulation. Generosity enables us to become our best selves.

How easy is it for you to give or receive? Write about your generosity in your WJ.

The Wisdom of Grace

Grace happens.

— From a bumper sticker

This bumper sticker is a variation on a popular saying. The noun that graces the more common observation is now frequently seen in print and heard from the lips of even the young.

We live in a society of believers in Murphy's Law: If something can go wrong, it will. Some people may have undergone conversion to the more rigorous sect characterized by Sullivan's Law — that the Murphy of Murphy's Law was an optimist. Of course, evidence abounds to bolster the argument that entropy and the Second Law of Thermodynamics exist in human affairs as much as in physics. One war is hardly over before two more start up. Irrational hatreds fuel racial and ethnic feuds lasting centuries. Things don't get better; they seem to get worse. We don't grow younger; we grow older. The good old days appear gone forever. And no one escapes death.

Yet grace does happen. The gifts originating in powers greater and wiser than ourselves are present 24/7. But like radio or TV waves, we will never see them without the equipment to make them manifest. This surely is why Jesus constantly harped on ears to hear and eyes to see and performed so many miracles curing the deaf and the blind. We consider something absent if we can't perceive it.

When we begin seeing with eyes of thanksgiving rather than eyes of blame, Murphy and Sullivan will start losing their followers. Then grace will visibly abound on the earth, and we will begin studying war no more.

In your WJ describe an example of grace you have experienced.

The Wisdom of Hard Work

So long as there is anything the superior person has not studied or cannot understand, he or she will never stop working.
— Confucius (551–479 BCE)

When I started learning Chinese 40 years ago, one of the first Mandarin words I memorized was *nu-li* (pronounced new-lee), which means "hard-work(ing)."

Mr. and Mrs. Li, my Chinese teacher and his wife, were visiting scholars from Shanghai. They were poor as church mice and lived gratis for several years at our church in exchange for custodial work. While studying for their Ph.Ds. in linguistics, the Lis worked at least three jobs: teaching Chinese privately, working in stores in Chicago's Chinatown, and conducting a low-level import business. They seemed to live on nothing, but occasionally they threw a nine-course party that would knock your socks off. How they could pull that off is still a mystery to me.

In a few years they were able to bring their then twelve-year-old daughter from China to live with them. After the Tiananmen uprising they were granted permanent residency. Around that time Li told me they had managed to amass a nest egg of $50,000.

Jawaharlal Nehru once said, "Life is like a game of cards. The hand that is dealt you represents determinism; the way you play it is free will." Although the Lis had been dealt a tough hand, they knew the wisdom and power of *nu-li*. Once in the States, they worked hard, soon reaping material benefits beyond what most native-born Americans would ever achieve.

How hard are you willing to work to reach your objectives? Write in your WJ about your work style.

The Wisdom of Kindness

What wisdom can you find that is greater than kindness?
                                    – Jean-Jacques Rousseau (1712–1778)

Those who have studied philosophy may recall that of the two great eighteenth-century French philosophers, Voltaire (1694–1778) epitomized the classical view while Rousseau, his younger contemporary, stood for the romantic. We might sum up the difference in this way: Voltaire-head, Rousseau-heart. It is thus not surprising to find Rousseau preferring kindness, a virtue of the heart, to wisdom, which seems more related to the intellect.

Buddhism, a sensible, balanced religion in many ways, holds *prajna* (wisdom) and *karuna* (compassion) as the two chief virtues of the fully realized human being. Buddhist life cultivates both wisdom and compassion, for without wisdom our compassion may be poorly directed, and without compassion our wisdom may be coldly intellectual. Although some Buddhist traditions give pride of place to one or the other, they are generally viewed as insufficient unless conjoined.

In some forms of Christianity, a similar tension exists between law and faith or works and grace. In the New Testament, St. Paul was the great champion of faith. St. James by contrast added works, as in this famous passage from his epistle: "For as the body without the spirit is dead, so faith without works is dead also" (James 2:26, KJV).

The difference between a cold, distant wise person and someone foolish but kindly is distinct. Rousseau, Buddhism, and Ss. Paul and James can help us see that true wisdom is always accompanied by compassion and kindness. Wisdom without kindness is both inadequate and unwise.

In your WJ discuss the kindest person you know and how they express their kindness.

The Wisdom of Learning by Doing

One must learn by doing the thing; for though you think you know it, you have no certainty until you try.
— Sophocles (c. 496–406 BCE), *Trachiniae*

Most college professors never learn to teach until they have jobs. Future schoolteachers are required to take a practicum course and do a year of student teaching, but those preparing for the professoriate simply learn the subject matter. If they know and love it, the prevailing logic holds, they will be able to teach it. Basically, you're thrown into the water of college teaching, and from there on, it's sink or swim. For the sake of future students, one must hope for the best.

Actually, many of life's important functions are learned by doing them. Living with others, raising children, and managing time and money come to mind. No school that I'm aware of teaches these skills. We are left to learn from the good and bad examples in our lives. But we can also read self-help books, take personal-development workshops, join parent-effectiveness training groups, and consult financial planners.

The Hindu and Buddhist religions are based on the concept of sequential rebirth—to give each soul the time needed to learn all the lessons of human existence. Later relationships can also be better than earlier ones, as can business ventures. Certain things really are better the second time around.

The wisdom here is to realize that while to err is human, to forgive ourselves, learn our lessons, and do better next time is divine.

In your WJ describe an example from your life in which you learned something important by doing it.

The Wisdom of Love

There is no difficulty that enough love will not conquer; no disease that enough love will not heal; no door that enough love will not open; no gulf that enough love will not bridge; no wall that enough love will not throw down; no sin that enough love will not redeem.
— Emmet Fox (1886–1951)

As I write these reflections, I sometimes wonder whether I have left out some really important topic. Love wisdom, I thought, would certainly have been covered. Wrong! So here I am with dozens of essays done and only now getting to love.

The Latin motto we English majors learn when studying Chaucer is *amor vincit omnia*, "Love conquers everything." These three words summarize Mr. Fox's more elaborately stated point. I remember Erich Segal's related comment, which imprinted itself in our cultural memory, in his 1970 novel *Love Story* when a character says, "Love means never having to say you're sorry." The sense is that in loving relationships you show consideration by avoiding words or actions that would upset the beloved. Then, of course, there'd be no need to apologize.

Unfortunately, I have too often done things that have hurt others. It's not enough to rationalize, as I do, that I am just following the Golden Rule—that I would not have been offended in their place. Each person is different. One takes offense where another wouldn't, and vice versa. For me, saying I am sorry and promising to be more sensitive in the future strike me as loving ways of nurturing my relationships.

Discuss in your WJ what you do to maintain your intimate relationships.

The Wisdom of No

*The key to a healthy "no" is to remember the "yes" that the "no" is
making space for.*

– Alan Cohen

How hard it is to say "no"! We all want to be agreeable. In our
childhood, saying no was generally not an option. When we did,
it often didn't get us what we wanted and sometimes got us what
we didn't want, like being grounded for backtalk.

Yet the #metoo movement makes clear how important Alan
Cohen's "Healthy No" is. My wife, a psychotherapist, often advises
clients to have good boundaries. Many, she says, lack them, with
negative results for their lives. Unfortunately, as most of the
#metoo stories make clear, it's not easy to say no to a powerful
person, on whose favor a woman's livelihood depends. The men
here are the ones needing boundaries.

For my part, I frequently take on too much. Wanting to improve
the world and being conscientious, I am called on even in my late-
70s for some volunteer job. Fortunately, I am increasingly able to
say "no," usually followed by "but thanks for asking."

To be sure, there are little no's and big ones. Turning down one
more calorie-laden cookie or politely refusing a movie invitation
when you're tired exemplify the former. Saying no to drinking
before driving or investing in a questionable deal, the latter.

Recently Alan sent as one of his wonderful daily emails this
saying by Goethe (1749–1832): "As soon as you trust yourself, you
will know how to live." Apparently, trusting ourselves can help us
say a healthy no.

Write in your WJ about your capacity to tell someone no.

The Wisdom of Positive Thinking

There is nothing either good or bad, but thinking makes it so.
– William Shakespeare (1564–1616), *Hamlet*, II.ii.250

The Power of Positive Thinking and *How to Win Friends & Influence People* impressed me greatly in high school.

Both books made sense and, to the extent that I followed the ideas offered by the authors, Dr. Norman Vincent Peale and Dale Carnegie, they seemed to work.

Years later, when I was a college dean in Chicago, someone introduced me to Napoleon Hill's extraordinary *Think and Grow Rich*. I remember highlighting half the words in the book, then spending most of a Saturday entering excerpts into my old Apple IIe. At my next staff meeting we took an hour discussing Hill's wisdom and how we could apply it to our programs of adult, continuing, and nontraditional education.

As administrators at an urban university with many older, minority, and first-generation students, how could we not be inspired by Hill's heady words: "All achievement, all earned riches, have their beginning in an idea!" Or, "Whatever the mind of man [sic] can conceive and believe it can achieve."

Similarly, in *The Aladdin Factor* (1995) by Canfield and Hansen, we are told that we each have a powerful genie within, one that can do magic. We just have to learn how to call it forth.

I am American enough to love these authors' ideas, puritanical enough to fear their success, and religious enough to believe that by taking thought, I can do only so much. The rest is up to the Universe.

What are the possibilities or limitations of positive thinking? Discuss this question in your WJ.

The Wisdom of Practicing the Presence of God

He had attained a state wherein he thought only of God... He gave no thought to those things he had finished with and almost none to those in which he was engaged... but all [things] were done very simply... to keep him in the loving presence of God.

– The Abbe de Beaufort on Brother Lawrence of the
Resurrection (1614–1691)

Brother Lawrence, a French Carmelite lay brother, never wrote a book. He did develop a following for his everyday spirituality, however. After his death his abbot found some of Lawrence's letters, added his favorite sayings plus memories of conversations with Lawrence, and combined them into a slender volume, *The Practice of the Presence of God*, which became a bestseller among Christians.

Lawrence, born Nicholas Herman in Lorraine, France, came from a religious family. After fighting in the Thirty Years' War, he served as a footman in an aristocratic household. Soon he left for Paris to become a lay monk in a monastery where he spent the rest of his life. He worked first in the kitchen, then in the shoe shop. After ten difficult years, a peacefulness came that remained with him until he died.

According to theologian Henri Nouwen, prayer for Lawrence was not "saying prayers but a way of living in which all we do becomes prayer." Practicing the presence of God meant living in the present moment—following Jesus' advice to take no thought for the morrow. Should we try this too?

Practice living in God's presence for a day. Discuss the experience in your WJ.

The Wisdom of Significance over Success

It's not the what; it's the so-what.

– Alexander Maclaren Witherspoon (1894–1964)

A doctoral dissertation is supposed to be a work of original research. In reality, when you write a dissertation, you are adding your ideas to the work of others with different if related ideas. There are original ideas, but to explain them in the context of different ideas, you have to use the work of others. The construction you create may be unique, but the building materials are derivative, like so many Lego pieces.

This thought occurs as I borrow a saying from my favorite professor, the late Alexander Maclaren Witherspoon of Yale. The main idea of the saying—the privileging of significance over success—is itself derivative. I have heard it before and since.

Success is the what of our lives. Significance is the so-what. Many counsel us on how to become successful, generally through the acquisition of material things and personal wealth. Do this and become rich. Do that and win the wo/man of your dreams. I have nothing against gaining wealth or a wonderful partner, but these attainments beg the next question. Wealth for what? Or how will my partner and I spend our time together now that s/he has been won. In short, so what? What's the significance of my success? How do I score the points?

As we journey through life in our success-oriented culture, it might help to ask ourselves from time to time, "So what?"

In your WJ name two of your significant accomplishments to date. Do you see them as "so whats" or "whats"? Explain how you view them.

The Wisdom of Simplicity

What is wisdom? Where can it be found? … It can be found only inside oneself. To be able to find it, one has first to liberate oneself from such masters as greed and envy.
— E.F. Schumacher (1911–1977), *Small Is Beautiful*, 1973

Wisdom may be available to each human being, but it must be mined and refined. The problem is that we are both miner and minefield, purifier and that which needs purifying.

In the 1998 film *One True Thing*, William Hurt plays a narcissistic professor who likes to quote Schumacher's slogan "less is more." The irony is that it was *more* comfortable for Hurt's character to show *less* concern for his wife and children than they were required to show him. Greed, envy, and other self-serving behaviors were in evidence despite his popularity as a with-it literature professor who had come of age in the 1960s.

I don't think Schumacher, an established hero among Western liberal intellectuals in the 70s, would have recognized much of himself in that film character. Wisdom for Schumacher was the fruit of work on ourselves. We "disarm" envy and greed "by resisting the temptation of letting our luxuries become needs; and perhaps by even scrutinizing our needs to see if they cannot be simplified and reduced" (*Small Is Beautiful*). His is not the way of extreme asceticism but of ongoing self-monitoring. "Buddhist economics" was the term coined to describe this form of personal vigilance.

Write in your WJ about something you do now to keep your life simple. What are some other things you might do to simplify it even more?

The Wisdom of Speaking from Within

The essential thing is not what we say, but what God says to us and through us.
– Mother Teresa of Calcutta (1910–1997), *A Gift for God*, 1975

According to an old tradition, when we speak our best, it is not our ordinary self speaking but the Divine speaking within and through us. This is the literal meaning of *inspiration* (being filled with the spirit) and *enthusiasm* (having the God-force, *theos*, within). When we speak from this place, our listeners are rapt—caught up in the spirit—and moved.

Consider when Moses was about to be sent on his mission to Pharaoh. Moses complained to God that he, Moses, was "slow of tongue." How could he possibly persuade the Egyptian king to let the Jewish people go? God counseled him not to worry, for He, the Lord, would do the talking. Jesus similarly advised his disciples not to be concerned about what to say on their mission trips, because the Holy Spirit would give them the words that were needed. And in shamanic cultures, spirit-guides possess the adepts, enabling them to provide messages of prophecy or healing.

I have experienced something similar on two occasions: once as I was addressing a psychology class at a university in Jakarta and again during a professional lecture in St. Paul, Minnesota. In both cases I talked freely, as if from an invisible script another had prepared, while observing both myself and the audience. These were among the best, most effective talks I ever gave.

Have you ever felt inspired from within while speaking publicly or privately? Describe the experience in your WJ.

The Wisdom of Tithing

Every tithe on land, whether from grain or from the fruit of a tree, belongs to the Lord; it is holy to the Lord... Every tenth creature that passes under the counting rod shall be holy to the Lord; this applies to all tithes of cattle and sheep.

– Leviticus 27:30–32

I wonder what percentage of Christians or Jews tithe. A tithe (tenth) or less, I am guessing. It took me till age 75 to get with the program. The last three years, in fact, I've been able to go beyond ten percent by a couple of points.

Now you may argue that the ruling in Leviticus came well before public taxation. Each of us in America is taxed on income and purchases. Taken together, what we pay comes to much more than ten percent.

In the interest of sound living, it's good to simplify our lives and live within our income. Stewardship begins at home. One of my former pastors, the late Doug Olson of Calvary by the Sea Lutheran Church in Honolulu, suggested that everyone do a double tithe: one to the church and the other to themselves. If we give to God and ourselves first, we are forced to live within the balance. Meanwhile the church is strengthened, and before long we have income-producing assets that can sustain us while guaranteeing a financially acceptable retirement. Now why didn't I acquire this wisdom when I was twenty? Fortunately, the angels in charge of the mildly improvident seem to be giving me a pass so far.

Write in your WJ about your habits of personal and charitable stewardship.

The Wisdom to Enjoy Life

There are two things to aim at in life: first, to get what you want; and after that to enjoy it. Only the wisest of people achieve the second.

– Logan Pearsall Smith (1865–1946)

The true scarlet letter in our puritanical culture is E for enjoyment. We are praised for working hard and honored for doing well. But we often feel guilty about relaxing and having fun. The commandment we break most, I think, is the fourth. Interestingly this injunction that we honor the Sabbath and keep it holy takes up more verses in Exodus (20: 8–11) than any other commandment. Christian ministers are the worst offenders, I joke with my pastor friends. They routinely profane the Sabbath by working.

One rare Sunday I didn't work. I made a deliberate choice not to turn on the computer or look at my e-mail inbox. "On six days thou shall be glued to thy computer to earn thy daily bread, but on the seventh thou shall lay back, have fun with thy friends, eat pizza, even go to the movies," said an inner voice tired of my workaholic ways.

The real sages are those who not only know how to relax on weekends but who marble their work week with time-outs, playful moments, and purposeless activities. I refer to these mini-sabbaticals as putting holes into the Swiss cheese of life. Unfortunately, when it comes to personal time management, I tend to buy my Swiss cheese in blocks.

Have you "lettered" yet on the enjoyment team, or are you too busy to slow down and enjoy life? Discuss this question in your WJ.

The Wisdom to Know the Difference

God grant me the serenity to accept the things I cannot change, the courage to change the things I can, and the wisdom to know the difference.
　　　　　　– Reinhold Niebuhr (1892–1971), "Serenity Prayer"

I am blessed with several recovering alcoholics in my family — blessed not because they are alcoholics but because they have been sober for many years and have built solid, responsible lives through participation in Alcoholics Anonymous.

In fact, I am twice blessed. Many years ago I joined Al-Anon, a Twelve Step program for friends and families of alcoholics. We practice the same program as AA members. The difference is that we keep the focus on ourselves, not the alcoholic. We learn how to build up our own lives and recover who we really are.

Among Al-Anon's tools are attending meetings, practicing the Twelve Steps and Traditions, doing daily readings, hooking up with a sponsor (an established member who can serve as a coach), internalizing the slogans ("easy does it, one day at a time, let go and let God," and so on), and practicing prayer and meditation.

Most famous of all these is probably the Serenity Prayer, which is often used to open and close meetings and is printed on commemorative medals. This prayer is certainly helpful for handling life's challenges. Circumstances beyond our control must be accepted. However, bad situations that can be changed should be. The real trick is knowing which is which. Therein lies wisdom, and serenity.

During the coming week, whenever you are in a tight spot, recite the Serenity Prayer to yourself. Write about the effects of this practice in your WJ.

Timeless Wisdom

Dear God... we must accept that time always brings change; and we pray that by your grace the change within our souls will make us worthy of your heavenly kingdom, where all time will cease.

– Alcuin of York (c. 735–804)

I look into the mirror these days and see my father. Talk about the changes wrought by time! Inside, of course, I feel as young as ever. I think the Roman poet Ausonius (c. 310–396) had the right idea about growing older when he wrote, "Let us never know what old age is. Let us know the happiness time brings, not count the years." The reality seems to be that our inner self is somehow ageless, while our outer self grows old and dies.

Christianity's view, represented here by Alcuin of York, an 8th-century teacher and poet, has traditionally placed greater value on the eternal life of the spirit than the temporary life of the body; on heaven rather than the earthly abode where moths corrupt and thieves break in and steal (Matt. 6:19).

Alcuin's prayer implies the need to put first things first and live in time as in eternity. That is, while we of course live in the days and years of our lives here and now, we also remember that we are, as the saying goes, spiritual beings having a physical, earthly experience. In that light, let us accept God's transforming activities within us as we would the coaching of a personal trainer and do our real work.

What does the passing of time and the changes it brings mean to you? Respond in your WJ.

True-Philosopher Wisdom

To be a philosopher is not merely to have subtle thoughts... but so to love wisdom as to live according to its dictates, a life of simplicity, independence, magnanimity, and trust.
— Henry David Thoreau (1817–1862), *Walden*, 1854

Philosophers are professional lovers of wisdom. That's what the word means in the Greek. And we doctors of philosophy have acquired that love, one assumes, with a responsibility to pass it on to our students and others.

During my junior year in Germany, the Yale faculty sagely let me do whatever I wanted. They thought that just by being in an area teeming with culture, I would learn at least as much as in New Haven's competitive classrooms. Not trusting their permissiveness, I read through a trunk-load of books; kept a 500-page journal in English, German, and French; traveled extensively; and discussed politics, history, philosophy, and religion in cafes and restaurants in Germany and elsewhere across the Continent.

By living in other cultures, I gained profound insights into who I was as a Jew, an American, and a human being. I learned that of the three, the last had the most profound claim on my identity. My European experiences presented many opportunities that made me older and wiser. When I returned to Yale, I was pleasantly surprised to receive "honors" for my work. My professors were amazed at how much I had done. Although I was still a year away from my B.A., I had taken a big step on my path to becoming a true philosopher.

In your WJ explore your philosophy of education by writing about a special learning experience.

U.N. Wisdom

The U.N., whose membership comprises almost all the states in the world, is founded on the principle of the equal worth of every human being.
– Kofi Annan, U.N. Secretary General, 1997–2006

The Preamble to the U.N. Constitution (1945) states, *"We the peoples of the United Nations have determined to save succeeding generations from the scourge of war... [and] have resolved to combine our efforts to accomplish [this aim]."* I could never understand Americans who thought this document ranked with the *Communist Manifesto* as a product of Satan. The minute we shift a little loyalty from the red-white-and-blue to the U.N.'s blue-and-white, the fat is on the fire. Everything previous generations of Americans have worked for would be lost, these individuals seem to say.

Really? What could possibly be wrong with a world without war? Or, as the Preamble continues to say, a place where everyone's human rights are respected? Where promises between nations are kept? Where we all work together for the economic and social well-being of each? Where, as the eighth Secretary General, Ban Ki-Moon, urged us, we become global citizens, act with passion and compassion, and help make this world safer and more sustainable both today and in future. That, Mr. Ban argues, is our moral responsibility.

We can be citizens of both our state and the United States. So why not of both the United States and the world?

The U.N. Charter and what Messrs. Annan and Ban say sound remarkably like mainstream Judeo-Christian ethics—like the Golden Rule. What could be wiser than that?

Discuss in your WJ the promise and dangers of internationalism.

Unconditional-Love Wisdom

I don't want someone who sees the good about me. I want someone who sees the bad and still loves me.

— Source Unknown

How fortunate I was to have someone who personified this sort of wisdom in my life when I was very young! It wasn't my parents, although as I grow older and hear about my friends' parents, mine look increasingly better. No. It was Florine Tolson Bond, our housekeeper, known back in the early 1940s as "the colored maid."

Florine had come to us in Great Neck, Long Island, from my mother's twin sister, Helen, in Philadelphia. Aunt Helen and Uncle Sol, the family dentist, had no kids. So when my mother, after a hiatus of nearly nine years, delivered me, my aunt sent us Florine for a year to help my mother out. I was one-and-a-half or two. She never left until I had graduated from high school.

It was love at first sight for both of us. Florine called me "Man" or "my Man"; my father "the Boss"; my mother "the Miss"; and my sister by her name. She hummed hymns in her kitchen; introduced me to The Mills Brothers and The Ink Spots, both of whom she called "the Boys"; told me about Jesus; corrected me with kindness; and loved me unconditionally.

At her request, my father invested part of her wages in blue-chip stocks. Childless herself but well-off, she put her nieces and nephews through college. Hundreds attended her funeral. The only white person there, I rode in the family car. I was Florine's son.

Write in your WJ about someone who showed you unconditional love.

Unexpected Wisdom

For those who fear
Allah, He (ever) prepares
A way out,
And He provides for him
From (sources) he never
Could imagine.
— The Koran, Surá LXV, 2–3, Abdullah Yusuf Ali Translation

I learned this lesson in 1958 as an exchange student in Germany. Before school started, another American student and I did some traveling. Our last stop was Munich.

On a dreary autumn day, we visited the nearby village of Dachau. The German government had not yet erected a memorial at the camp. In fact, after arriving we had no idea how to find it and didn't want to ask. After wandering around, we stumbled on a U.S. military post. "It's here," the M.P. said.

Douglas and I were the only visitors. At one point, alone, I encountered two pizza-style ovens, their doors wide open. Spontaneously I put my right index finger through the grate and, with the ash, drew a capital "J" on the back of my left hand.

The next day, on the express back to Heidelberg, two middle-aged men entered our compartment. They asked us about ourselves. My friend answered he was a German-American student. "I'm an American exchange student too," I said, "but my ancestors were Jewish." They protested their ignorance of the camps. I didn't care about them. I had carefully hidden my Jewishness during my four months in Germany—afraid how people might react. I had concealed it even in the States. Suddenly I remembered the day before. These martyrs had not died totally in vain. Thanks to them, I never denied my Jewishness again.

In your WJ write about something that occurred beyond your expectations.

Unlimited-Capacity Wisdom

What do we teach our children? ... We should say to each of them: Do you know what you are? You are a marvel. You are unique... You have the capacity for anything.

— Pablo Casals (1876–1973)

Consider this: Children shouldn't be encouraged to become *whatever* they want. Rather, they should grow into the unique individuals they already are. That person may turn out to be a skilled furniture restorer or a talented chef or a juice-bar owner like my goddaughter. Or something else altogether. Why always a Mozart or President of the United States?

Come to think of it, why do we tend to equate a successful life with one's profession? Why should all the points go to being famous and none to a person's quality as a human being? A parent? A son or daughter? A friend?

A young friend of mine, just 24, is a brilliant writer and photographer. She is also beautiful and nice. Right now, though, both her education and career are on hold while she cares for her mother who has terminal cancer. If anything, she is increasing her capacity.

Considered one of the greatest cellists of all time, Señor Casals is really talking about not foreclosing children's options. In former times and still today in some cultures, your individual potential was limited not by capacity but by society. If persons in your caste were merchants, you would have to be one too. In this regard I prefer the U.S. Army's slogan: "Be all that you can be."

In your WJ share how you think children should be encouraged concerning their future.

Utopian Wisdom

He [Joachim] is the most important apocalyptic thinker of the whole medieval period, and maybe after the prophet John, the most important apocalyptic thinker in the history of Christianity.

– Saintscatholic.blogspot.com

Born in 1130 or 1135, the Blessed Joachim was known, among other things, as Joachim de Flore, Joachim of Flora, Joachim the Prophet, Joachim von Fiore, and Gioacchino da Fiore. A mystic and theologian, he founded a monastery in southern Italy, was a favorite of popes and kings—including Richard the Lionheart—and was venerated by Dante and the Franciscans. After his death in 1202, however, virtually all his ideas, especially his main one on the Holy Trinity, were declared heretical by the Catholic Church.

So, what did this prophet say that so inspired individuals and upset Church officials? In short, he claimed to have had a mystical experience through which the real meaning of the Holy Trinity was revealed to him.

The Three Persons—Father, Son, and Holy Spirit—actually signified for him three successive ages. The first, the Age of the Father, stood for obedience to the divine law in the Hebrew Scriptures. The second, the Age of the Son, indicated life under the Gospel through the vicarious atonement of Christ. The third, the Age of the Holy Spirit, would be that utopian age when everyone would come to know Divinity from the inside out, with peace and harmony the result. As God says in Jeremiah 31:34, "All will know me, from the least to the greatest… and I will no longer remember their wrongs" (GNB).

Write in your WJ about your ideas of a utopian age.

Vacation Wisdom

A little work, a little play,
To keep us going — and so, good-day!
— George Du Maurier (1834–1896)

Nature instructs us in the wisdom of balanced living seasoned with variety, the proverbial spice of life. First this, then that. Never always the same thing: shifts in the seasons, variations in the weather, the succession of night and day, sleep following wakefulness. Yet out of our tendency to work too much and our fear of being unable to do it all, we ignore the need for downtime and "non-productive" play, let alone for vacations.

Play may just be the most productive activity around: the breathing out that makes the breathing in possible. As we must work for our vacations, so our vacations enable us to keep working once we're home again. "All work and no play makes Jack a dull boy," Poor Richard counsels. And employers want a dull worker about as much as a chef wants a dull knife.

"Okay," you respond. "I already know all this, and I try my best to take periodic vacations with my family." Good for you. But plenty of people out there, like me, intersperse work with more work. In doing so, we are proof for the observation that we preach to others the very things we should practice ourselves. Come to think of it, I am writing this essay during my vacation. However, I am about to throw on my swimsuit and go to the beach. Right now I am on the Island of Kauai, after all.

Do you make sure to get away periodically? Write in your WJ about one of your best vacations.

Walking Wisdom

Caminante no hay camino, se hace camino al andar.
(Walker, there is no path; the path is made by walking.)
                              – Antonio Machado (1875–1939)

"Hola, Peregrino." "Greetings, Pilgrim." We are all walking this sacred way called life, but each of us has to make his or her own path. We are headed not toward Santiago de Compostela in Antonio Machado's Spain but to the Temple of Santa Sofia, the place of Holy Wisdom. Come, let us walk together for a while on *this* Camino.

Beginning August 23, 2017, my wife, Cedar Barstow, and I set out to walk the 200 kilometers, 120 miles, from Villafranca del Bierzo in Leon Province to the Cathedral of St. James the Apostle, legendary Christian missionary to Spain, in Santiago de Compostela, a smallish city in the northwestern Spanish Province of Galicia. We were following in the footsteps of millions of pilgrims who'd been walking this path since around 800 CE. Ours was the Camino Frances, the French Camino, which begins in Paris. It was the best known of many similar paths, all marked with yellow arrows pointing the way. Both in our 70s, we were overjoyed to reach our destination ten days later.

Sharon Clark and I have offered you these little essays to point the way to your own wisdom. At the end of each, as you have seen, there's a writing prompt to help you do that. When you're done, your Wisdom Journal (WJ) may contain more words than this book. For now, *Buen Camino!* May your pilgrimage to more life wisdom be blessed.

In your WJ reflect on what wisdom means to you now.

Wealth Wisdom

For many people the acquisition of wealth does not end their troubles; it only changes them.

– Seneca (4 BCE?–65 CE)

In our materialistic culture, money is supposed to be the golden road to the good life. If only it were as easy as Ben Franklin's "Early to bed and early to rise makes a man healthy, wealthy, and wise."

While wealth can help us avoid worries about paying the bills, even that goal may elude us if we live beyond our means. Wealth also attracts problems that less affluent people rarely have. No one marries you for your money, for instance, if you don't have any.

A 1990s miniseries depicted the unhappy life of Doris Duke, heiress to the Duke tobacco fortune. And the late J. Paul Getty, who at one point was the richest man in the world, wrote an essay entitled something like "It's Not Easy Being a Billionaire," where he said he could never have a trusting relationship. His concern was always that others were out for his money.

It's wise to understand that wealth is not a one-way ticket to happiness, even if we have the winning lottery number. What would we do with that much money? What would our choices say about our values? Contentment tends to come, if at all, in spite of our wealth or lack thereof.

If you were wealthy, what would you do to avoid the sorts of problems that dogged Doris Duke and J. Paul Getty? Sketch out a strategy in your WJ. If you are wealthy, write about whether you are happy and what you might do to live more contentedly.

Wisdom as Panacea

The only medicine for suffering, crime, and all the other woes of mankind [sic] is wisdom.

– Thomas H. Huxley (1825–1895)

Can this profound statement from a Victorian biologist be true? Isn't a part of wisdom knowing that there is no "sure cure" for our worldly problems? A famous pessimist like the writer of Ecclesiastes goes so far as to say "in much wisdom is much grief" (1:18). So how could wisdom possibly cure all our ills?

Huxley was an agnostic and a prominent defender of Darwin's theory of evolution. He would probably have agreed with his future brother-in-science Dr. Jonas Salk, who wrote that evolution is now calling for a critical mass of human beings with the capacity to make life-affirming decisions. He felt that global survival would depend on it (*The Survival of the Wisest*, 1973). For Salk, wisdom was the human capacity to make judgments which over time proved beneficial to self, others, and the planet as a whole. Presumably he was talking about enlightened public policy and helpful social practices. Interestingly, Dr. Salk, like Huxley a fellow agnostic who never talked about God, always capitalized the word *evolution*.

Perhaps we can take Huxley's statement that "wisdom is the only medicine" at face value and pray for a modern-day Dr. Salk to develop a Wisdom vaccine, just as he was working on one for AIDS at the time of his death. If he mixed in daily doses of compassion and optimism, surely we could cure all the woes of humankind.

In what ways might wisdom improve the human condition? Write for ten minutes on this topic in your WJ.

Wisdom as You

Wisdom is the experience of your own nature. It is the expression of your self-being. It is the flowering of your own consciousness. It is not information, it is transformation.
    – Rajneesh, as quoted in a Noetic Sciences brochure

I first heard about Bhagwan Shree Rajneesh when he was being deported from his ashram in Oregon on federal tax-evasion charges. The media saw him as a typical East Indian cult leader, a guru playing on the needs of innocent young Americans while stealing their money and youth.

But two of my colleagues, both with doctorates from prestigious universities and enviable careers, were "Rajneeshis" for a while. One lived for several years in a group-marriage situation and made recreational use of marijuana. The other, one of the most dependable people I know, followed the master to India and lived there as a celibate for a time. Yet a third colleague forwarded the above quotation to me. In the intervening years, now in Boulder, Colorado, I have met three more responsible individuals, all of whom feel they learned a great deal from the person they call Osho, his *aka*. Who or what to believe about Rajneesh? I'll accept the wisdom of the quotation.

Like other spiritual leaders from India, Rajneesh emphasizes the immanence of wisdom. We each carry our own supply. So, while wisdom is available to each of us, we must exercise our spiritual muscles to access and use it. It may be there for the taking, but we must work hard to acquire it.

Discuss in your WJ how you tap your own nature in order to experience personal transformation.

Wisdom from Failure

For the pure scientist, a failed experiment is no failure at all but a vital step toward learning the truth.
— Parker J. Palmer, *The Active Life*, 1991

In our success-oriented culture, failure can be a fate worse than death. There are stories of ex-millionaires throwing themselves from Wall Street windows after losing fortunes in the 1929 stock-market crash. How can there be wisdom in failure?

Sharon and I as authors know the famous failure-to-success story of the *Chicken Soup for the Soul* series. These books have now sold over a half billion (!) copies worldwide. According to co-author Jack Canfield, "Many, many people said that *Chicken Soup* would never work as a book." By the time the first book appeared, it had been rejected by 144 publishers. When finally accepted by a small self-help publisher in Florida, that person thought selling 20,000 books would be a reach. The rest, as the saying goes, is history.

In the world of entrepreneurship, similar stories abound. Through failures we can build an eventual pathway to success. Failed businesses help us see what needs to be done better to achieve profits. Failed relationships, if properly understood, can equip us for doing better in the future. Jobs that don't work out can give us insight into our true talents and enable us to know the sort of work that will be best for us. My belief is that our Higher Power guides us with "No" as well as "Yes." Wisdom comes from understanding failure as often the best springboard to success.

In your WJ discuss a "failure" that ended up helping you to a better life.

Wisdom in the Schools

Life's tragedy is that we get old too soon and wise too late.
— Benjamin Franklin (1706–1790)

I wish wisdom were taught from the earliest grades in schools. Once I was asked to talk about wisdom with an 11th-grade AP English class. I started by saying that *"wisdom* comes from two English words, *wise* and *dumb."* They laughed. I continued, "If you get an A on your final, is that wise or dumb?" "Wise!" came the unanimous reply. "What if you dive into an empty swimming pool?" "Dumb!" they groaned.

I then confessed that our word *wisdom* actually comes from the Latin *visio* (sight) and the Old English *deman* (Mod. English *deem,* to judge). The word really means making decisions based on taking into account all aspects of a situation. Poor decisions result in poor actions — bad marriages, dysfunctional parenting, unfortunate business deals, and harmful public policy. My hope was that after the class, the students would think about wisdom and its role in their lives.

We are here on earth to learn to be truly human, to fulfill our potential, to respect all other life, and to live in accordance with our highest spiritual promptings. Wouldn't it be helpful to introduce the concept of wisdom early on in formal education? That way students would learn that attempting to live wisely is among the most important things we human beings can do.

What's your opinion about making wisdom a required topic in school curricula? Do you think you would have lived more wisely if you had learnt more about wisdom during your formative years? Reflect on this subject in your WJ.

Wisdom Is as Wisdom Does

Two Hasids were discussing their weekend plans. One said, "I intend to visit the great rabbi in Lvov." "To hear his words of wisdom?" his friend inquired. "No, to see how he ties his shoes."
– Adapted from Martin Buber (1878–1965), *Tales of the Hasidim*, 1947

Talking a good game is relatively easy. When I went to college, we called it "a snow job." In fact, some of us thought college was all about learning to do bigger and better snow jobs—on parents, on girlfriends, on future employers. Impress them, we believed, and we would get our way.

Great wisdom, the first Hasid implies, manifests in the small change of daily living. We are as we do, not as we say. Buckminster Fuller wrote a poem entitled "God Is a Verb." *Natura naturans* was how Renaissance writers put it in Latin: freely, "Nature doing its thing."

Personal transformation—the journey from our smaller, more foolish self to our larger, wiser one—is a prime goal of all the world's religious and spiritual traditions. The secular equivalent is self-improvement.

If we are faithful to who we are, then who we are will affect what we do. In short, wisdom does as wisdom is. So, to act wisely, we have to become wiser so that wisdom comes to guide our daily life. The trick is learning to trust our inner guidance. I hope this book is giving you some tips.

Who is the wisest person you know? Describe this individual in your WJ. What makes her or him wise? How might you apply some of their "wisdom style" to your life?

Wisdom of the Tao

Five hundred years before the birth of Jesus, a God-realized being named Lao-tzu in ancient China dictated 81 verses which are regarded by many as the ultimate commentary on the nature of existence. The classic text of these verses offers advice and guidance that is balanced, moral, spiritual, and always concerned with working for the good.

– Wayne W. Dyer (1940–2015), "How I Discovered the Wisdom of the Tao," 2015

Tao, pronounced "dow" in Mandarin, is the ideogram (concept-picture) for "road" or "path." It shows someone moving along, looking as they go. The character is used metaphorically for any doctrine or intellectual way.

The Chinese are a practical people, as the ideogram suggests. It's one thing to espouse a philosophy but another when you actually set forth and act on your beliefs. An agrarian people for thousands of years, the Chinese understand that patience is the first requisite of the good farmer. A Chinese proverb, quoted by Confucius, cautions against pulling on young rice shoots to make them grow faster. Natural processes have their own rhythms which we disregard at our peril.

An excellent student is one who can correctly assess the value of something and act accordingly. After a year studying the Tao, Dr. Dyer wrote a book on the wisdom of living in alignment with Nature.

The wisest among us will understand this message and follow the path of Tao, much as some of Jesus' first disciples left whatever they were doing to follow him. Whoever has ears, let them hear.

Read something from the Tao Te Ching; *then spend five minutes writing a response in your WJ.*

Working Wisdom

Give me, dear Lord, a pure heart and a wise mind, that I may carry out my work according to your will... Above all, remind me constantly that I have nothing except what you give me and can do nothing except what you enable me to do.

– Jacob Boehme (1575–1624)

When Martin Luther translated the Bible into German, he hoped to make the Scriptures and religion more broadly available. He helped found compulsory public education, because most German speakers in his day were illiterate. As a Catholic priest and Augustinian monk, he was also careful to preserve and translate parts of the Mass for reading at the appointed times in church.

Jacob Boehme, born ninety years after Luther, was a shoemaker from Saxony. The religious controversies of his day enraged him. A Protestant, he believed the path to God lay in contemplation. Boehme considered that anyone, by going within, could receive the sorts of experiences described in the Bible and could write personal prayers.

St. Ignatius of Loyola (1491–1556) introduced this paradox: "Pray as if everything depended on God, but work as if everything depended on you."

Boehme takes the mystical position that everything depends on God and that one must therefore totally surrender to the divine will.

Most important is that we figure out what our work is and do it; serve others as we've been served; and acknowledge the Great Life Force, our forebears, and our teachers as the sources of all we have and do—including our capacity to work.

What does "working wisdom" mean to you. Discuss in your WJ whether you side with Loyola or Boehme and why.

World-Citizen Wisdom

Socrates said he was not an Athenian or a Greek, but a citizen of the world.
> – Plutarch (c. 46–120), "Of Banishment"

I don't understand why some people dislike the idea of humankind coming together to form a single global nation. Maybe it's because we Americans have worked hard to develop a prosperous country and comfortable lifestyle. If we had a global government with democratic representation, we might be outvoted by the many countries less well off. They could then end up taxing away our prosperity to improve their own lot.

The United States is perhaps the most successful example of a multiregional nation. Many regions—the West Coast, the South, New England, the Lower and Upper Midwest—could be nations unto themselves. We are also a multiethnic country where soon people of color will be more numerous than their Caucasian counterparts. Yet we live together in relative harmony. So why not a United States of the World?

The answer is, we need a critical mass of world citizens like Socrates to establish a viable global nation. Ethnicity and religion per se are not the problem. In Hawaii the population is two-thirds non-white, and there is a significant Buddhist minority. Still they manage to live together in peace, have perhaps the highest cross-racial marriage rates in the world, and are famous for their Aloha Spirit.

Even issues of language and distance will fade once most of us outgrow the adolescent chauvinism and provincialism dominant in today's world. We will then exemplify the motto of the World Future Society by thinking globally while acting locally.

Discuss your views of world citizenship in your WJ.

World-Healing Wisdom

Each of us has a unique part to play in the healing of the world.
— Marianne Williamson

Spiritual teacher Marianne Williamson is one of the primary spokespersons for A Course In Miracles, a self-study spiritual program. The philosophy on which the Course is based informs her talks, seminars, and books, including four *New York Times* bestsellers. She also founded a charity, Project Angel Food, which serves food to homebound individuals with AIDS in Greater Los Angeles. And, through The Peace Alliance, an organization she cofounded, she continues to lobby the U.S. Government to create a Department of Peace. Clearly, Marianne is doing her part to heal the world.

According to the website myjewishlearning.com, the Hebrew phrase for healing the world, *tikkun olam*, originally a mystical concept associated with the Kabbalah, now connotes social-action programs as well as individual and collective works of charity and kindness. It underlies the commitment of many Jews and Christians to charitable causes and to being good stewards of the earth.

Political activist Rabbi Michael Lerner edits the progressive Jewish magazine *Tikkun*, which also advocates for interfaith understanding and cooperation on actions that would help heal (*tikkun*) a fragmented and violent world (*olam*). A rabbi in the Jewish Renewal Movement founded by Reb Zalman, Lerner recently wrote an editorial calling for an end to the occupation by Israel of the West Bank. This position looks to balance the concerns and needs of Palestinians *and* Israelis. The larger point, however, is that each of us is responsible for helping to *tikkun olam*—to heal our world.

Discuss in your WJ what part you now play in healing the world.

Write-Myself-a-Letter Wisdom

I'm gonna sit right down and write myself a letter...
— A 1935 song by Fred E. Ahlert and Joe Young

Wisdom, I've been saying, is our inner guidance system. Although it concerns something out there, the direction we get comes from in here. The question is, how do we access that wisdom? How do we get it to emerge?

There are lots of ways. Here's one I've experienced.

First, I sat down and meditated. I placed my awareness on my breathing and followed it for about three minutes. Then, I thought of an issue I'd been wrestling with for some time—something where the pros and the cons had resulted in a kind of hung jury. I just could not come up with a decision.

Next, I wrote myself a letter in which I, that is, my BIG I, gave me some advice. I wrote, "Dear Reynold" at the top of a blank sheet. I wrote my name in the normal way with only the first letter capitalized. Then I wrote freely. At the end, I put down "Love" and—this is important—signed my name again, this time with all capital letters: "REYNOLD."

I went on to use this technique successfully in workshops around the world. Inevitably, someone would come up at the end to say that the advice received had solved a long-standing problem as it had for me. Our deep inner knowing can be magical. I turn to it regularly for guidance.

Follow the instructions above with some challenge in your life. Write your letter in your WJ. Then briefly comment on the process and results.

Commencement Wisdom

In my end is my beginning.
– The motto of Mary Stuart, Queen of Scots (1542–1587)

Commencement is a word that looks two ways. During my student days, it denoted the end of a course of study, a recognition that I had completed all requirements for a degree and was ready to move on. The word also has to do with new beginnings. The familiar expression says it all: "Today is the first day of the rest of your life."

Commencement wisdom is knowing that Divinity makes everything new and that we, as co-creators, have the opportunity each moment to begin again. Yesterday we may have *graduated*, a word that means "having taken a step." But today we are called on to graduate again.

It helps to acknowledge the successful completion of each day. It is also sensible to break life up into a series of present opportunities. This strategy is contained in the Twelve Step slogan "One day at a time." Letting bygones be bygones, starting afresh, celebrating the accomplishment of having reached this new day, week, month, or year is a formula for wise living.

So, as you conclude this book, know that the future will give you daily chances to live a wiser life. If you have discovered inner wisdom to help you along the way, these essays will have served their purpose.

Sit quietly, then leaf through your WJ. Let thoughts and images come and go. After a few minutes, do one more WJ exercise: Write three things you intend to do in the future to live more wisely. Best wishes as you are guided by your inner wisdom.

Acknowledgments

It *does* take a village to do almost anything these days. So, the two of us would like to thank the many people, living and dead, who have contributed to these pages. First, there are the wise individuals we have quoted. Then there are the many people in our past and present who said or did something which modeled a particular form of wise living, examples which have found their way from our hearts into this book. Special thanks to our endorsers for the kind things they said about *Wisdom for Living*.

Thanks are also due to our publisher, John Hunt Publishing and O-Books, with special regard for Maria Barry, our publicist there, and to Cate Colburn-Smith, our marketing consultant in Colorado.

Neither of us could have completed a project like this without the support of those near and dear to us. Sharon's thanks go to Ren (Reynold Feldman) for his willingness to collaborate and to her friends and teachers who have inspired and supported her writing efforts. Thanks from Ren go to Dr. Cedar Barstow, Marianna Levine, Harper Levine, Dr. Christine Feldman-Barrett, Richard Barrett, Margaret Pevec, Arisa LaFond, Ana Paula Bastian, and the men of the Lafayette (CO) men's group for their consistent good faith and support.

Next, we'd like to thank each other. Writing a book together can test a relationship. We are thus grateful that those stresses and strains, along with occasional bursts of enthusiasm, have made our friendship and ability to collaborate even stronger.

Finally, we thank you, our readers. We hope our little book inspires you to live a wiser life from within.

Sincerely,

Reynold Feldman & *Sharon Clark*
Boulder, Colorado & Novato, California
Fall 2018

BOOKS

SPIRITUALITY

O is a symbol of the world, of oneness and unity; this eye represents knowledge and insight. We publish titles on general spirituality and living a spiritual life. We aim to inform and help you on your own journey in this life.

If you have enjoyed this book, why not tell other readers by posting a review on your preferred book site? Recent bestsellers from O-Books are:

Heart of Tantric Sex
Diana Richardson
Revealing Eastern secrets of deep love and intimacy to Western couples.
Paperback: 978-1-90381-637-0 ebook: 978-1-84694-637-0

Crystal Prescriptions
The A-Z guide to over 1,200 symptoms and their healing crystals
Judy Hall
The first in the popular series of six books, this handy little guide is packed as tight as a pill-bottle with crystal remedies for ailments.
Paperback: 978-1-90504-740-6 ebook: 978-1-84694-629-5

Take Me To Truth
Undoing the Ego
Nouk Sanchez, Tomas Vieira
The best-selling step-by-step book on shedding the Ego, using the teachings of *A Course In Miracles*.
Paperback: 978-1-84694-050-7 ebook: 978-1-84694-654-7

The 7 Myths about Love...Actually!
The journey from your HEAD to the HEART of your SOUL
Mike George
Smashes all the myths about LOVE.
Paperback: 978-1-84694-288-4 ebook: 978-1-84694-682-0

The Holy Spirit's Interpretation of the New Testament
A Course in Understanding and Acceptance
Regina Dawn Akers
Following on from the strength of *A Course In Miracles*, NTI teaches us how to experience the love and oneness of God.
Paperback: 978-1-84694-085-9 ebook: 978-1-78099-083-5

The Message of A Course In Miracles
A translation of the text in plain language
Elizabeth A. Cronkhite
A translation of *A Course in Miracles* into plain, everyday language for anyone seeking inner peace. The companion volume, *Practicing A Course In Miracles*, offers practical lessons and mentoring.
Paperback: 978-1-84694-319-5 ebook: 978-1-84694-642-4

Thinker's Guide to God
Peter Vardy
An introduction to key issues in the philosophy of religion.
Paperback: 978-1-90381-622-6

Your Simple Path
Find happiness in every step
Ian Tucker
A guide to helping us reconnect with what is really important in
our lives.
Paperback: 978-1-78279-349-6 ebook: 978-1-78279-348-9

365 Days of Wisdom
Daily Messages To Inspire You Through The Year
Dadi Janki
Daily messages which cool the mind, warm the heart and guide
you along your journey.
Paperback: 978-1-84694-863-3 ebook: 978-1-84694-864-0

Readers of ebooks can buy or view any of these bestsellers by
clicking on the live link in the title. Most titles are published
in paperback and as an ebook. Paperbacks are available in
traditional bookshops. Both print and ebook formats are
available online.

Find more titles and sign up to our readers' newsletter at
http://www.johnhuntpublishing.com/mind-body-spirit

Follow us on Facebook at https://www.facebook.com/OBooks/
and Twitter at https://twitter.com/obooks